The 50 Mile Bouquet

# THE 50 MILE BOUQUET

*Seasonal, Local and Sustainable Flowers*

**Debra Prinzing** | **Photographed by David E. Perry**

Foreword by Amy Stewart, author of *Flower Confidential*

St. Lynn's press

PITTSBURGH

**The 50 Mile Bouquet**
Seasonal, Local and Sustainable Flowers

Copyright © 2012 by Debra Prinzing and David E. Perry

Text by Debra Prinzing; Photography by David E. Perry

ISBN-13: 978-0-9832726-4-9

Library of Congress Control Number: 2011944665
CIP information available upon request

First Edition, 2012

St. Lynn's Press • POB 18680 • Pittsburgh, PA 15236
412.466.0790 • www.stlynnspress.com

Book design – James Forkner, Studio Bolo
Editor – Catherine Dees

Additional photos: page 83 (center right), by Debra Prinzing;
page 143 (top), by Mary Grace Long.

Note: Captions for photographs on the front and back covers,
title page and table of contents are shown on page 144.

Printed in The United States of America

This title and all of St. Lynn's Press books may be purchased for educational,
business, or sales promotional use. For information please write:
Special Markets Department • St. Lynn's Press • POB 18680 • Pittsburgh, PA 15236

10 9 8 7 6 5 4 3 2 1

**Debra:** To my husband Bruce Brooks, whose love and belief in me is more cherished than all the bouquets I'll ever gather.

**David:** To Dad, who has always encouraged me to love the questions as much as the answers.

# Contents

# Slow Flowers...or 50 Miles from Home

Several years ago, I found myself traveling around the world talking to flower growers and florists about the dazzlingly beautiful – and perplexing – business of flowers. How did something as natural and ephemeral as a flower spawn a global industry? And what, if anything, had we lost along the way?

One chilly Monday morning in 2007 I met Teresa Sabankaya in Santa Cruz, California. Right away she seemed like a kindred spirit – a Texas girl like me, with a generous smile and an obvious love of the outdoors. She'd found a way to take her excessively abundant garden and turn it into a business, selling flowers from a stall on the street and doing arrangements for weddings and special occasions. Even though she'd expanded her inventory to include flowers from around the world, she still bought locally. She told me about a gardener who regularly offered her surplus flowers. "She's just some lady, you know?" Teresa said. "She'll pull up in front of the shop with a car full of beautiful flowers. I buy whatever she's got."

That conversation made a big impression on me. I was in the middle of investigating a giant industry run by large corporations for my book, *Flower Confidential.* I had seen flowers grown in factories, stored in warehouses, shipped by truck and plane. I had seen supermarkets buy bouquets from Latin America and sell them by the thousands as a loss-leader. What I had not seen, until I talked to Teresa, was a passion for seasonal, local flowers that look like they came straight out of the garden – and often did.

A great deal has changed since *Flower Confidential.* The notion of supporting local farmers was just gaining traction. The idea of celebrating our seasonal abundance – even if that means giving up tomatoes in January – was not quite mainstream. Just as "slow food" was catching on, the flower world was beginning the shift that *The 50 Mile Bouquet* celebrates.

When Debra and David began interviewing and photographing people who grow and arrange fresh, seasonal flowers for local markets, I knew they were documenting a new movement…you could call it the slow flower movement. I'd already been meeting a generation of young, optimistic flower growers who were motivated by their love of flowers and their commitment to sustainable farming. Some of them were in their early twenties; they'd just gone out and rented a few acres of land, covered it in manure, and planted flowers. No one told them that the flower business didn't work like that anymore, that today's flowers didn't grow in soil, didn't see the sun, and weren't visited by bees and butterflies. Fortunately, they followed their passion anyway.

The stories and images in this book lead us forward, to a new way of enjoying unfussy, chemical-free, natural flowers. But they also take us back to our grandmothers' gardens, and to the flower farms that used to surround every city, offering sweet peas in spring and dahlias in late summer and cherry blossoms in February. There's nostalgia in these pages, but there is also a decidedly modern sensibility and an undercurrent of excitement over what the future holds for farmers, florists, and flower lovers like me.

Many people who read *Flower Confidential* told me they never looked at a flower the same way again. If you're ready to rekindle your passion for flowers, *The 50 Mile Bouquet* will take you there – and "there" might be no farther than your own backyard. Enjoy the journey.

– Amy Stewart, *New York Times* best selling author

# Follow Your Flowers from Field to Vase

Do you enjoy flowers in your life? Are you drawn to a voluptuous heirloom rose like a bee to honey? Is burying your head in a just-picked garden bouquet and inhaling its perfume a joy-inducing experience? You are not alone. Our love affair with flowers is ancient and visceral. But lately something has been missing from everyday flowers – you've probably noticed. That clutch of gerbera daisies or tulips from the supermarket may appear picture-perfect, yet it feels disconnected from the less-than-perfect (but incredibly romantic) flowers growing in your own backyard. The mixed bouquet delivered in a happy-face vase by a floral service is pretty enough,

but somehow looks unnatural, as if it were produced in a laboratory and not in real garden soil, nurtured by sun and rain. These blooms feel far removed from the fields in which they grew. And they are, in more ways than one. To the many of us who seek that visceral joy of just-picked bouquets to bring into our homes or use for special celebrations – or give as gifts to others – the flower has lost its soul. What happened?

These are "factory flowers," grown by a $40 billion worldwide floriculture industry whose goal is uniformity and durability – so as to withstand long shipping distances. They are altogether different from the carefree zinnias, romantic peonies and wispy cosmos you clip from the garden for a home-styled arrangement. The $100 box of long-stemmed roses may look close to perfect, but its contents have been off the farm for up to two weeks. Those scentless creations were likely grown a continent or two away and shipped on a dose of preservatives to travel to you – poor substitutes for heady, abundant armloads of blooms gathered from grandmother's cutting garden. They have lost the fleeting, ephemeral quality of an old-fashioned, just-picked bouquet.

## A Greener Way

"Green" floral design is only recently appearing in the sustainable living lexicon, but the term suggests using flowers that have been grown with eco-friendly methods. To us, it feels authentic, echoing the voices of those in the slow food movement. Why can't we have flowers that come from local fields? Or ones that express the cycle of seasons? Isn't that a more natural, and sustainable, way to bring flowers into our lives?

**Above:** The fading allure of field-grown tulips is a reminder of the fleeting nature of a garden flower. They are to be enjoyed and cherished in the moment.

**Opposite:** Diane Szukovathy of Jello Mold Farm in Washington's Skagit Valley is a sustainable grower whose practices are safe for the earth, the flowers she plants and the people who ultimately enjoy them. She brings blooms from the field to market within 48 hours of harvest, to the delight of floral designers and flower lovers alike.

**Previous spread:** A French rose, this lovely light pink variety is called 'La Fraicheur'. It blooms in the garden of rose aficionado Anne Belovich, who prefers ramblers and climbers to the modern hybrids.

Faced with concerns about our food supply, the materials with which our homes are built and furnished, and the energy sources we consume, more people than ever are asking questions about the environmental impact of everything they use, drive, eat and even wear.

And yet, until recently, conscious consumers were largely unaware of the decidedly non-green attributes of their floral purchases. They bought bouquets without questioning the source, or the manner in which those flowers were grown (not to mention the environmental costs of shipping a perishable, luxury commodity around the globe). When presented with the real back story of their bouquets, some have initially said, "I don't eat my flowers, so why should I care if they are organic or not?" or "How damaging to the earth is a $10 bunch of cellophane-wrapped mums anyway?" For others, it's been a revelation.

Take the idea of buying local: In the world of foods, the concept of "eating local" has become accepted in our culture. Many of us already embrace the premise that "local" is desirable, over non-local. According to a statewide study by the California Cut Flower Commission, 85 percent of consumers did not know where the flowers they purchase are from; however, more than half (55 percent) indicated they would purchase flowers grown locally, in California, if they were given the choice.

**Above:** The heady scents, evocative color and romantic appearance of old-fashioned lilacs are perhaps the quintessential symbol of springtime.

**Right:** Berkeley-based designer Max Gill creates soulful arrangements for Alice Waters' renowned Chez Panisse Restaurant & Café. He uses wild-foraged ingredients, vines and branches from his city-sized garden and blooms grown by Bay Area flower farms.

It's our belief that many consumers want to bring home blooms that are fresh, local and safe. Even though hard data on the harmful effects of pesticides and other chemicals used in the commercial floral trade have been slow in coming, anecdotal evidence from our interviews with organic flower farmers, green floral designers, and retailers who market sustainably-grown flowers supports our belief.

Whether or not they consider themselves environmentalists, consumers are beginning to exercise their choices at the flower stand, asking whether the beautiful roses, lilies or tulips they purchase at the local supermarket were grown domestically or were imported. They are looking for labeling that guarantees flowers have been produced in an environmentally and socially responsible manner – finding it in an increasing number of outlets as diverse as Sam's Club, Trader Joe's, Whole Foods and the neighborhood grocery store.

More flower shops and wedding designers are marketing themselves as "organic, local and sustainable," seeking healthy, artful ingredients grown in their own communities by small family farms. As demand for green flowers increases, the sources of chemical-free crops will also expand, allowing the local flower farmer to earn a living wage supplying designers, florists and consumers in his or her own community. Seasons change, and so do the varieties, offering us the pleasure of celebrating the full cycle of a calendar year in the garden. But seasonality does not

mean giving up our floral traditions. There are lovely, domestically-grown roses available to buy and give on Valentine's Day – but only for those who are intentional, insisting that the florist source Oregon- or California-grown roses for holiday giving. And of course, you can embrace the moment differently, such as giving your beloved a pot of hyacinth blooms that have been forced indoors.

As more flower consumers pose the questions: "Is this local? ... Is this seasonal? ... Is this sustainable?" – we've heard them. We've collected the answers to those questions and more in the pages of *The 50 Mile Bouquet.* Here you'll find inspiring and creative resources and how-to ideas, techniques and information to enjoy flowers in your daily life, even if you aren't a gardener.

Planning a wedding? We'll introduce you to floral designers who work with local farmers to create unforgettable, one-of-a-kind bouquets for your day of days. Planning a special event that cries out for fresh flowers, but you live in an area with limited access to fresh, locally-grown blooms? We'll put you in touch with domestic flower farmers and florists from other areas who can ship your orders overnight.

**Above:** In the back of a flower farmer's van, buckets of blooms resemble a vibrant tapestry. From grasses and gourds to sunflowers and dahlias, the diversity of field-grown ingredients is sure to delight – and inspire – the floral designer who receives this delivery.

Our book aspires to be the essential resource for savvy, eco-conscious consumers who may be aware that the flowers they buy at the corner market or order from a local florist or wire service are not organic, but who need a road map to guide them to better – and more beautiful – alternatives. Rather than pointing to the perceived lack of choice or limitations of the floral industry, *The 50 Mile Bouquet* will empower and equip gardeners, flower enthusiasts, floral designers, event planners and their customers to take a proactive, informed approach to the flowers in their lives and work. Consider this the "slow flower" guide to organic flower growing, gathering and design.

## A sustainable rose by any other name

Recently, a reader of our blog asked: "I have always bought local. What I don't understand is the term 'sustainable.' Can you expand?" Before we even had a chance to post an answer or define the term, another reader shared her point of view as an urban flower farmer and designer. Jennie Love owns Philadelphia-based Love 'n Fresh Flowers. She wrote:

"I am a small flower farmer in Pennsylvania who grows organically, but is not certified as 'organic' due to the debilitating high costs of going through the (USDA) certification process. So I use the words 'sustainably grown' to describe my flowers (due to government regulations, if you're not a Certified Organic operation, you cannot use the word 'organic' in promoting what you produce). What 'sustainably grown' means to me is this in a nutshell: *being careful to not take more from the land and the community than I am putting back into them.*

"In my daily farming practices, I am using cover crops, compost, all-natural fertilizers, good watering practices, limited tilling of the land, lots of native plants so the local insect population has food sources, nurturing old antique/heirloom flowers that might not necessarily be money makers but are going to disappear from our world if growers like me don't keep using them, and generally being very thoughtful about how everything I do in the field is going to impact not just that field but the forest that surrounds the field, the underwater streams that run from the field to the rivers, and the flora and fauna in that field and elsewhere in 5–10 years. And I never use synthetic chemicals to fight bugs or weeds.

"In my business practices, I work hard at engaging and educating my immediate community – literally my neighbors – and the city in which I live. I try to always be transparent about what I am doing and what my goals are when people ask about my business. I have recently hired my first employee and I am paying well above minimum wage (more than I can afford, really) and providing flexible work hours that fit into his schedule so his quality of life improves because he is working for me. I make a point to donate lots of flowers to different non-profits and to nursing homes. . . .

"Most importantly, to me at least, is that I have a rule: My flowers never go further than 75 miles from where they grew. I want my flowers and my business to enrich the lives of those who live around me in as many ways as possible. To me, that's giving back more than I take from this world."

**Above:** Look to your own backyard to find seasonal ingredients for a simple arrangement. Photographer David Perry transformed a cube of landscaping sod into a green pedestal that showcases his vase of ephemeral spring garden flowers, including bluebells *(Scilla non-scripta)*, bleeding hearts *(Dicentra formosa)* and snowflakes *(Leucojum aestivum).*

We were so impressed with Jennie's eloquent and respectful response. She highlighted some of the challenges small flower farmers face when it comes to the nuances with definitions and labeling of organic products definitions. The myriad terminology is helpful to learn, and you'll see that in the pages of this book, we sometimes use "organic" with a lower-case "o" to differentiate from Organic, as defined by the United States Department of Agriculture. To learn more, please check out the useful section on Sustainability Terms, page 140.

## Change Your Relationship with Flowers

In the pages that follow, you will meet flower farmers, supermarket flower buyers, floral designers, wedding planners, farmers' market vendors and creative DIYers who are committed to growing, selling and designing with a "green" approach. This is a book that engages the senses. Feast your eyes on the evocative photo portrayals of these "slow flower" pioneers. Get lost in the images of both the uncommon and the everyday – buds, blooms, branches, leaves and berries – as they grow and are ultimately used by floral artists. We invite you to read the intimate narratives of every person we've met on our floral journey, including the growers who are passionately committed to sustainable practices and the designers who use ingenuity and innovation to source their ingredients locally and seasonally – and eliminate conventional and often harmful industry practices. Follow with us as we tell the story of *The 50 Mile Bouquet,* as it travels from field to vase.

We hope that this book connects you with a healthier, flower-filled lifestyle, one that helps you engage with nature, with the environment, and with the very blooms you desire. Enjoy safe and sustainable flowers, the ones you grow yourself in a cutting garden or the ones in pots on your balcony. Gather bouquets with your children, not worrying that they'll come in contact with pesticides. Share those bunches with a neighbor who doesn't have a garden. Source fresh blooms from flower growers in your own community, whether you live in the town or country. And finally, learn how to design with confidence, as you create personal, evocative bouquets of your own. It's a better way to beautiful.

*– Debra and David*

**Above:** Breathtakingly beautiful, the summertime arrangement designed by Erin Benzakein of Mt. Vernon, Washington-based *floret* includes heirloom roses, garden geraniums and ornamental alliums cut from Waverly Jaegel's lush, Skagit Valley landscape.

**Next spread:** Flower farmer Joan Ewer Thorndike of Le Mera Gardens holds an armful of just-picked ranunculus and anemones in colors so pure they take one's breath away.

# CHAPTER ONE

# Portrait of a Flower Farmer

*"When I sell my flowers, I believe I am appealing to my customer's deeply visceral desire to observe the cadence of Nature."*

**– Joan Ewer Thorndike,**
Le Mera Gardens

# WITH LOVE, FROM SKAGIT VALLEY

## Cut flowers sustainably grown

Blackberries, rose hips, pea vines, chestnut tree branches – perhaps not the bouquet ingredients you would expect to find at your local supermarket or even an upscale florist. But flower farmers **Diane Szukovathy** and **Dennis Westphall** view everything that grows on their eight-acre farm in Washington's verdant Skagit Valley as a potential element of a gorgeous centerpiece or gift bouquet.

The husband-and-wife team spent more than a decade creating elegant residential gardens in some of Seattle's toniest neighborhoods. Yet they yearned to own land and support themselves as farmers. "We needed to do something that fed our souls," Diane explains to us on our visit to their farmstead. Diane laughs easily, her eyes bright through smart-chic lenses, her long blonde braid swinging across her back as she moves. You might think Dennis is the shy member of this duo, until he grabs his guitar and sings a song he composed about recycling – a nod to his other calling as founder and director of Tickle Tune Typhoon, a much-loved and nationally renowned children's music company.

Eleven years ago, Dennis and Diane moved 60 miles north of Seattle to the semirural agricultural community of Mt. Vernon. Their initial plan was to establish a Community Supported Agriculture (CSA) operation and raise food crops for subscribers. That changed when, after volunteering with a local organic vegetable grower, the couple discovered that the economics of edibles wouldn't work for them. "We couldn't make our mortgage growing food," Dennis says.

Admittedly a pair of "plant freaks," he and Diane instead sowed flowers, filling their fields with perennials, annuals, ornamental grasses and flowering shrubs for the florist market. Jello Mold Farm takes its name from Diane and Dennis's original business, Jello Mold Landscape, which was inspired by a crazy building in Seattle's Belltown neighborhood that Diane once covered with 400 copper-hued Jello molds of all shapes and styles. Now, several of those shiny forms – starbursts, crescents and domes – adorn the farm's outbuildings, adding a bright glimmer to the landscape.

Their hearts, souls and the intense but satisfying labor of 14- to 16-hour days are poured into growing 150 varieties, including decorative edibles like grapevines, crabapples, Cinderella pumpkins and heirloom squashes. Eight hundred peony shrubs and fifteen hundred dahlias produce an endless supply of gorgeous, romantic stems during peak season.

To these flower farmers, the term "sustainably grown" means a commitment beyond just using organic fertilizers and chemical-free pest control techniques. Diane and Dennis consider themselves land stewards who share their acreage with an array of wildlife. The hedgerows, thickets and native trees provide an important bridge into the farmland for many animals, including trumpeter swans, bald eagles, ospreys, several kinds of owls, hawks and songbirds. "We work hard to keep the soil healthy," Diane explains. "That way, the critters make a living and so do we. Sustainability for us means leaving the land in better shape than we found it." Jello Mold is certified Salmon Safe, a regional designation recognizing agricultural land that is safe for watersheds.

**Above, from top:** Skagit Valley's wildlife, including a white-crowned sparrow, finds habitat along the uncultivated margins of Jello Mold Farm's growing fields. The farm's sustainable practices mean no chemical treatments are used on the soil or the plantings; beneficial insects like spiders feast on pests that otherwise damage ornamental crops. This natural cycle of pest control occurs without human intervention or chemicals – and as a result, a healthy equilibrium is maintained.

**Opposite:** Diane Szukovathy and Dennis Westphall infuse their fields and crops with passion, playfulness and a sustainable business philosophy. In doing so, they inspire their customers to desire and value locally-grown floral ingredients.

Jello Mold Farm began supplying Seattle area flower markets in 2007, attracting interest from floral designers and wedding planners. Soon the business added a number of retail florists and the Ballard Market, a neighborhood grocery store whose floral buyer recognized a renewed sense of nostalgia and customer interest in locally-grown sources. Best Buds, a tiny flower shop in an upscale Seattle neighborhood, was the first to sign up for Jello Mold's twice-weekly deliveries. "Their customers know that our flowers are local and fresh," Diane says, "because we pick only one or two days before a delivery."

As advocates for sustainable flowers, Diane and Dennis have a high-touch approach. They tell a story about each alluring bloom and its must-have attributes, enticing floral designers to embrace unusual ingredients for their color, form or fragrance. In turn, the bouquets and arrangements designed with Jello Mold's flowers are uncommonly beautiful and sophisticated. Those who use conventional flowers or foliage are eager to enliven their designs with Jello Mold's offerings, such as the ninebark shrub, which has sultry maroon foliage; or a spray of blushing raspberries; or ruby silk grass, with red tassels on tall stems.

**Above, from top:** Ninebark *(Physocarpus opulifolius)* is a deciduous shrub that produces stunning reddish purple, copper or green foliage, depending on the cultivar. The unusual colored stems and foliage are popular with floral designers looking for a creative alternative to ordinary greenery; the sheer diversity of rare shapes, textures and colors grown by Jello Mold Farm is awe-inspiring, including the purple-streaked cardoon in the foreground.

Selections reflect the fleeting nature of botanical ingredients, the inevitable seasonal changes that Jello Mold Farm celebrates rather than resists. Twice a week, Diane emails an availability list to her Seattle-area customers. The "Fresh List" informs and inspires, with items described almost poetically: *"Atriplex (Orach) – plumes of colored seed pods, available in bright green and deep maroon-red"*... *"Chasmanthium (Northern Sea Oats) – shimmering green flattened seed heads with tall stems,"* or *"Shoo-Fly – unusual Chinese Lantern relative, bright green lanterns with purple-black crown, multi-branching."*

These tempting descriptions gladden the hearts of flower buyers who yearn to add local flavor to their designs. Stems are gathered into "grower's bunches" of five to 10 per cluster, secured with a long twist-tie on which is printed the farm's web site and location. The tie itself is a subtle marketing and educational effort, and it has prompted retail customers to begin asking for Jello Mold's flowers by name.

Diane and Dennis infuse grower's bunches and mixed supermarket bouquets with "something special that will surprise people," she says. "Our quality is fabulous and I want people to remember that. It's our best calling card. Fresh and local sells."

Even though sustainable farming practices can increase production costs, the farm isn't always able to charge more for its floral products. Jello Mold basically matches the prices buyers expect to pay at the major wholesale market where most product arrives from around the world, having been harvested more than a week earlier and likely treated with fumigants in order to clear U.S. Customs. Proclaiming "Our flowers are safe to sniff," Jello Mold subtly educates customers about the benefits of buying sustainably-grown, non-imported blooms.

The market is changing, though, with a new understanding among wholesale buyers that there is value-added benefit to sourcing from local flower farmers. Buyers are also motivated by demand from the end consumer, who is beginning to understand the health benefits (for themselves and the planet) of bringing home an organic, sustainably-grown bouquet. "It's in the food movement already," Diane says, "and the floral trade and their customers are catching up."

This momentum has been fueled in no small part by the opening in April 2011 of a cooperative called the Seattle Wholesale Growers Market, for which Jello Mold Farm is a founding member, with Diane serving as market president. Housed in a central Seattle location, a collective of 20 flower growers from Washington, Oregon and Alaska, sell direct to wholesale customers (see pages 24-29 for the full story).

**Above:** Jello Mold raises many types of garden roses for bouquets, but some unique varieties are planted for the sensational, cherry-red hips they produce come fall.

**Opposite, bottom:** A foggy morning on a working flower farm. While Diane and Dennis make their living from the land, they also consider themselves environmental stewards of their farm, their crops and the creatures who coexist here with them.

" *Some years ago, we were gardeners in the city with a romantic notion of having a farm," they say on Jello Mold's web site. "Little did we know the reality! Now we're knee-deep in paradise, and lovin' it."*

The spirit of collaboration with fellow growers expands beyond the region, as Jello Mold Farm shares flower-farming techniques and marketing ideas through the Association of Specialty Cut Flower Growers, a trade group. Thanks to an ASCFG research grant, Jello Mold Farm has experimented with methods to extend the growing season, allowing the farm to plant earlier in the spring and harvest later in the fall. For example, growing inside a hoop house allows Diane and Dennis to raise sweet peas, anemone, ranunculus and other spring crops a full month earlier and to grow sunflowers until the first week of November, much later than if they were left in the fields uncovered.

Additionally, the couple has introduced flowers and other botanical ingredients that the floral industry rarely sees, much less uses in its designs. "We're in the education business," Dennis points out. The farm maintains a trial garden of new cultivars and varieties, tracking when and how plants bloom, as well as how they perform in the vase.

At Jello Mold Farm, growing flowers in their season is both a philosophy and a savvy business strategy. But this approach also means the farm's most productive window occurs from March to November. To expand their ornamental offerings during the winter months, Diane and Dennis are adding cool-season offerings, such as cardoon foliage, winter-blooming camellia, witch hazel branches and ornamental willow. Climate, weather, and seasonal issues including the length of daylight, work to the farm's advantages in summer and spring, but leave the late fall and winter less productive. That's when planning, research and preparing for the following season also takes place.

Each season witnesses a new crop of excited wholesale clients, which Diane finds encouraging. "As consumers value the health benefits – to themselves and to the planet – of bringing home a sustainably-grown bouquet of flowers, demand grows." Farmers like Diane and Dennis have anticipated this demand, and are more than ready to satisfy it.

**Above:** With his wife and business partner Diane Szukovathy, flower farmer Dennis Westphall brings passion, playfulness and a sustainable business philosophy to his work. In doing so, he inspires customers to desire and value locally-grown floral ingredients.

**Opposite:** Diane carries on her shoulders a bounty of just-harvested *Helenium,* a rustic-looking perennial reminiscent of wildflowers.

## Jello Mold Farm's Top "Uncommon" Cut Flowers

Artichokes and Cardoons *(Cynaria)*

Chestnut Branches *(Castanea)*

Coral Peonies *(Paeonia* 'Coral Charm', Coral Sunset', 'Coral Supreme')

Crabapple Branches

False Indigo *(Baptisia australis)*

Fruiting Quince Branches *(Cydonia)*

Globe thistle *(Echinops)*

Hellebores *(Helleborus orientalis)*

Lupine *(Lupinus)*

Ornamental Grasses

Poppy Pods *(Papaver somniferum)*

Raspberry Foliage with young berries

Shoo-fly *(Nicandra physalodes)*

# Brimming with Blooms

## A gathering of growers under one roof forms a dynamic and cooperative market

A seed germinates when it comes in contact with light, warmth and the nourishment of healthy soil. Similarly, good ideas sprout and take root when they are sown in ideal conditions. That was how the Seattle Wholesale Growers Market Cooperative came into being – a new farm-to-market enterprise that connects cut flower farmers with florists and their customers.

On a sunny day in June, 2010, about 60 growers and floral designers gathered in the bucolic fields of Charles Little & Co.'s farm on Seavey Loop Road outside Eugene, Oregon. They stood near a hand-lettered U-Cut Flowers sign where Charles and Bethany Little raise and sell oodles of flowers, foliage, branches, pods and berries – 200 varieties – for the cut flower trade.

They were there for a regional meeting of the Association of Specialty Cut Flower Growers (ASCFG). The collective knowledge of these lively minds and generous souls was nothing short of amazing. While the straw-hatted crowd spent a day discussing the practical aspects of their craft and trade, something else was also going on. A seed of an idea was planted during the afternoon's informal "shop talk." Led by

Judy Laushman, ASCFG executive director, and Diane Szukovathy, a regional director for the organization, the dialogue centered on the challenge of farming flowers. One grower shared data on her best-selling Mother's Day crops (peonies and tulips); another told of her experiment with social media tools to attract local customers to her farmers' market stall.

But beyond individual successes, many growers acknowledge a desire to band together as a cooperative selling unit and create a "buy-direct-from-the-farmer" marketplace. They discussed possible formats already in existence, including one just 60 miles to the north, where the Portland Flower Market has thrived since it was started in 1942 by the Oregon Flower Growers Association. And they considered another interesting model: Fair Field Flowers, a popular Wisconsin venture that operates a direct-to-florist delivery van on behalf of 10 local farmers. Among the hopeful faces and earnest voices, there was a cadre of both established and relatively new flower farmers who said: "Let's do this in Seattle."

## A growing passion

Only a few months later, in October 2010, **Janet Foss**, a 30-year veteran farmer who has sold her beautiful floral crops everywhere from a rural roadside stand to Seattle's famed Pike Place Market, hosted an exploratory meeting at J. Foss Garden Flowers, her Chehalis, Washington, homestead and farm.

"We all had a vision to set up similarly to the Portland Market," Janet recalls. "Our goal was to give flower farmers a place to sell direct to florists, wedding and event designers, and other wholesale customers like grocery stores."

Along with Janet Foss, Diane Szukovathy and Dennis Westphall of Jello Mold Farm, **Patrick Zweifel** of Oregon Coastal Flowers, and **Vivian Larson** of Everyday Flowers formed the initial core group. Planning moved quickly into action, as the farmers took a study tour of the Portland Flower Market, where Charles Little & Co. has sold for more than a decade, and Oregon Coastal Flowers has sold since 2004.

By early 2011, with each of 12 original members investing $500 seed money, the Seattle Wholesale Growers Market Cooperative was formed. The energetic group began negotiations for a 4,000-square-foot warehouse in Seattle's hip Georgetown neighborhood. Ironically, the location was just blocks from the city's largest wholesale floral market, where the majority of cut flowers sold in the region arrive from around the globe, having traveled through the Vancouver, B.C., floral auction house, where commodity flowers are sold to bidders up and down the West Coast.

**Above:** Flowering dogwood branches in shades of coral, white and the palest of greens are harvested from Oregon Coastal Flowers. Floral designers gobble them up for stunning, early springtime arrangements.

**Opposite:** Dahlias representing the warmer end of the color spectrum are sorted and bunched by color and form. They bring brilliance and joy to the otherwise rugged loading dock at the Seattle Wholesale Growers Market, awaiting pickup from a busy florist. These were grown by Dan Pearson of Dan's Dahlias in Oakville, Washington.

"We knew the Seattle Wholesale Growers Market could offer a viable alternative to the imported flowers," Diane says. "This model has worked for years in Oregon, because the local flower farmers have a place to sell their crops – at the Portland Flower Market. By opening our own market here in Seattle, we're bringing the best local supply direct to the florist – and we believe this effort will be very beneficial to our local economy and to local agriculture."

## Pushing Petals

By April 2010, the market's "soft" opening took place. To some, it was an inauspicious beginning, since an extra-cold, wet spring delayed harvest for many of the members. But the heady scents of Oregon-grown lilacs and romantic bunches of antique-pink and pale green hellebores from Washington's Skagit Valley filled the exposed-brick warehouse space with sensory pleasures. Eight months after their initial discussions, this small band of flower farmers achieved its goal. "We wanted to be an indoor, year-round market with a modern edge," Diane says. "Pulling our group together to cooperate has created a great environment for people who love flowers to connect.

And now we have a central place to sell our products."

Making a living by growing and selling flowers requires horticultural knowledge, long hours and an ability to react quickly to everything from capricious weather conditions to fickle floral designers. But having a community of like-minded growers means the difference between success and failure for so many, says Vivian Larson of Everyday Flowers, based in Stanwood, Washington. "Everybody has taken a risk. We've gone to an uncomfortable place and stepped outside our boundaries. Technically, everyone here is a competitor, but we're operating from a good-business point of view, and we all feel that it's best to take care of our customers first."

This means, for example, that when Vivian's Everyday Flowers has a big wedding client, she knows Diane and Dennis at Jello Mold Farm will help her complete the order of specific quantities by selling her some of their own flower inventory. "It makes a happy customer, who leaves knowing that our market has what she needs," Vivian says, summing up what is the unspoken mission of the venture.

## Meet the Farmer

Ultimately, it's not just the excellent quality of fresh, sustainably-grown blooms, branches, stems and pods that is helping this emerging flower market gain new customers. With her sleeves rolled up, her glasses pushed to the top of her head and her arms filled with joy-inducing

dahlias, Vivian proclaims: "I think it's important to have the face of the farmer connected to these flowers." While the market operates four mornings a week, opening at 6 a.m. for early shoppers, Wednesday is the Market's "Grower Day," when most of the vendor-farmers come to the co-op.

Similarly, Vivian adds, it's helpful for the farmers to meet the flower buyer. "I love hearing from my buyers about how much they love my flowers and how long a specific bloom lasts in an arrangement. I want to know if something doesn't perform well as a cut flower, because then I can give that designer a credit or replace her flowers."

Two-way conversations also help floral designers gain product knowledge, which, Vivian feels, "gives them a way to differentiate themselves from their competitors. So many consumers don't realize where their flowers come from, but the florist can pass that information on to their clients. They can say: 'This was grown by a small farm in Skagit Valley,' and tell a story of each flower to the bride or hostess."

The personal touch is essential to staying competitive in a rapidly changing industry selling a perishable product. By using the SWGMC as a place to try out new crops and solicit feedback from designers and wholesale customers, each grower involved has gained new marketplace knowledge.

"This market has changed my whole way of thinking as a flower farmer," Janet Foss says. Perhaps one of the group's most pragmatic members, she speaks about the market with buoyant optimism, her eyes widening to make a point. "I've learned what people in the city want, people who are used to having more choice and variety. For example, I know I need to grow more sweet peas in the winter. And now, I'll always grow Queen Anne's lace, because designers love it."

Less than one year after launching, the cooperative's membership expanded to nearly 20 flower growers, including those with Oregon, Washington, and Alaska farms. There is a front desk manager and the selling floor is full of breathtaking botanical beauty, every season of the year. This means you'll see more flowering branches and evergreen foliage than warm-season perennials during the winter months, but like a chef who turns a turnip into a delicious winter stew, there is an ever-increasing community of savvy floral designers willing to work with what each season has to offer on the flower farm.

"We've proven that we can do this locally," Vivian says, a note of pride in her voice. "It's like our own little baseball field. We built it and they came. The thing that really makes us unique is that we are a group that works together. Not one of us could have done this alone – we all make each other better, and that's what a cooperative really is."

**Above, from top:** Dan's Dahlias grew this dazzling array of blooms. The farm is one of the most extensive dahlia sources in the region; the new wholesale market allows flower farmers and floral designers to meet, transact and learn from one another.

## External challenges

Patrick Zweifel's Oregon Coastal Flowers – his Tillamook, Oregon-based farm – has been well received by florists who shop at the Portland Flower Market, and at his permanent stall at the Los Angeles Flower Market District. Patrick's confidence and experience encouraged other farmers to invest in the Seattle-based cooperative venture. He is competitive by nature, bringing the intense energy that he once devoted to a college track and field career to his professional life.

"I knew there would be demand if we committed to the (warehouse) lease and took the risk," he says. "When you sell face-to-face, when you have a quality product, you have something that's so much better than what you see on paper or online." By opening their own market and direct-selling to florists, "we're cutting out the middleman," he adds.

But no matter how beautiful or fresh the bloom, domestic farmers face competition on price, especially from importers who buy from low-wage countries, Patrick says. "I was the first person in the U.S. to sell colored calla lilies in a big way. I couldn't have bought my farm without them. Then the South Americans started selling callas for 30 cents per stem against my $1-per-stem product. And they had added incentives, like buy one box, get a second one for free. Now, I just can't compete with South America on callas, even if my quality is great."

Patrick credits his ability to quickly change direction for saving his business. He noticed a few years ago that floral designers were snatching up his offerings of Northwest forest products, such as lichen-clad branches, soft green mosses, cone-laden conifer boughs and other woodland items, infusing their bouquets with a naturalistic feel. In the past three years, Oregon Coastal Flowers has increased the variety of specialty forest items, while at the same time shrinking its acreage devoted to calla lily production.

With forest service permits that allow him to legally harvest everything from birch saplings to decaying tree trunks, Patrick has recently seen his sales double. "I'd have been out of business if I didn't start doing this three years ago," he says. "You can't grow this stuff in South America, or even in too many places in the U.S."

## Generation Next

To raise startup funds and convert raw warehouse space into a functioning market, the SWGMC staged a two-day Growers School for would-be commercial flower farmers. "We realized that in many ways, our industry is young and could use education on quality growing and post-harvest techniques," Diane Szukovathy says. A partnership with Washington State University using WSDA Specialty Crop Block Grant Funding helped create the program, which drew 50 students to WSU's Mt. Vernon Research & Extension Center and later to Jello Mold Farm for field-demonstrations during two chilly February days. During one of the morning brainstorming sessions, the participants were asked, "Why grow flowers?" The responses ranged widely:

> To attract beneficial insects and pollinators
>
> To use and preserve farmland
>
> To be a "producer" and not a "consumer"
>
> To walk outside and be at work
>
> To be surrounded by beauty
>
> To diversify my food-growing farm
>
> To position flowers as the financial center of my farm
>
> To grow flowers for my own floral design business
>
> To improve the quality of life for my customers
>
> To include every generation of my family in the process
>
> To have a sense of community and know my neighbors

**Top:** Fifty new and established flower farmers toured one of the hoop houses at Jello Mold Farm as part of the Seattle Wholesale Growers Market's annual Growers School.

**Above:** The training involves a day of classroom time and a day of field study. By sharing their knowledge and experience with first-time flower farmers, the organizers of the Seattle Wholesale Growers Market feel they are investing in the long-term health of local flower farms.

The passion and motivation of flower farming is contagious. Many of the participants already raise and sell flower crops, but yearned to gain a deeper understanding of that "lost art" and "old wisdom" from experienced farmers. And as one generation teaches the next, the honorable profession of making a living from the land is preserved, one acre at a time.

# THE LAST ROSE FARM IN OREGON

## For three generations, the Peterkort family has produced beautiful roses domestically, despite relentless competition from South America

America's love affair with roses is inarguably the number one story in the floral world. According to the Society of American Florists, 196 million roses are produced for Valentine's Day alone. But only a fraction of them are grown domestically.

Most U.S.-grown roses hail from California, which accounts for 75 percent of the nation's output. Yet in Oregon, a small-scale grower called Peterkort Roses has been raising hybrid tea roses for the floral trade since the 1930s. The third-generation family farm currently produces 2 million roses annually, using many sustainable growing practices.

"We are an anachronism of the past," says **Sandra Peterkort Laubenthal**, granddaughter of Joseph and Bertha Peterkort, who came to Oregon from Germany and started raising flowers in 1923 on a portion of land owned by a farming cousin. "They originally grew gerberas, sweet peas and pansies. It was fortunate that they had five children to help with all that work."

During the 1930s they planted rose crops, beginning the family's long tradition with the flower that gave Portland its nickname, the City of Roses. Rose varieties with poetic names like 'Moonstruck' and 'Tara' comprise about 75 percent of the production, but Peterkort is also known for its gorgeous lilies, orchids, maidenhair ferns and ornamental holly. Sixteen greenhouses add up to six acres of flower-producing land.

In the past, Oregon was home to several commercial cut roses growers, but slowly, those operations have either shifted to other flower crops or folded altogether. "We have this certain niche, and we really want to support the local floral industry," Sandra says. "If there's going to be a local rose grower, it seems like the City of Roses ought to have one."

**Above:** Sandra Peterkort Laubenthal is a third-generation rose grower who brings modern-day "green" growing practices to the flower farm that's been in her family since 1923.

**Opposite:** 'Classic Cezanne', an ivory rose with mauve-pink edges, is just one of Peterkort's many popular varieties. Designers love the beautiful, just-harvested roses because they are easy to work with, last long in the vase and in bouquets, and are grown locally by people they know.

## Embracing change

As new-generation rose farmers, Sandra and her brother **Norman Peterkort**, the company's manager, face increasing competition from foreign rose growers, as well as rising energy costs at home. Says Sandra: "Our challenge is to find affordable ways to change with the industry and continue doing what we're doing." Where Sandra is outgoing and Norman is quieter, when you talk with them, it's evident that these siblings share a devotion to their flower-growing legacy.

Like many greenhouse growers, Peterkort uses a hydroponic farming system. Plants are grown above ground in a substrate, such as coconut fiber, which keeps the roots isolated in a controlled environment. Irrigation and rose food are delivered through micro-tubing direct to the plants' root zone.

Most roses grown for the cut flower trade are hybrid teas or related varieties that continue to produce flowers if they receive enough heat and light (versus old garden roses that are generally single-bloomers). In order to grow on a twelve-month cycle, Peterkort uses artificial light during months when daylight hours shorten, which does increase energy costs. "Admittedly, it doesn't make a lot of sense to be growing roses in the wintertime, but we're trying to be different from the competition," Norman points out. "While roses coming out of South America don't have heating costs, they do have transportation costs."

Price alone can't be used to compare Peterkort's 25-stem bunch of hybrid tea roses, which have a $20 wholesale price, with a similar number of larger Colombia-grown roses that wholesale for around $26.

"In the final analysis, a lot of people just buy on size," Norman acknowledges. "Yes, discerning customers will look at where the roses were grown and how they perform – and we can compete on that level, of course. We can't always afford to compete on price. If we want to survive we have to be better marketers."

By offering Northwest roses on a year-round basis, Peterkort satisfies floral designers and their customers who value locally-grown, natural-looking flowers. Changing taste levels have also helped drive demand, as was recently documented by a Society of American Florists report that the "fresh-picked" look, including wildflowers and garden roses, is on the rise among wedding customers.

## Homegrown roses

Peterkort's elegant blooms look vastly different from the softball-sized imported ones that consumers gobble up by the dozen every February 14th. Instead, the farm's 50-plus rose varieties are closer to what you might see gracing a mixed perennial border in the garden. Specialties include the classic hybrid tea rose, with upright, spiraled petals; a German-bred hybrid tea that features multi-petal characteristics of an old garden rose; and dainty spray roses with many tiny blooms on a single stem.

Designers count on Peterkort as an important local rose source for bridal bouquets, boutonnieres, flower girl wreaths and tabletop arrangements – available in a palette that begins with pure white roses and ends with ones bearing dark, velvety black-red petals. Unlike unscented imported roses, these have a light, pleasing fragrance. Because Peterkort harvests its flowers one day and sells them the next, the roses are super-fresh and, as a result, are long-lasting in the vase.

**Below:** Bunches of just-picked 'Peach Avalanche' roses showcase the variety's giant head, fluffy garden look, and greenish outer petals.

"I've been ordering roses from Peterkort for four years," says designer **Melissa Feveyear**, owner of Seattle-based Terra Bella Floral Design, who specializes in organic flowers. With varieties like 'Piano Freiland', a red, peony-shaped rose, and spray rose clusters that last several weeks in a vase, Peterkort's blooms make up in quality what they don't have in size, she says. Admittedly, the 1- to 2-inch flower head is nearly half that of an imported rose, but for many designers and consumers who prefer a softer, romantic bloom, this is not an issue.

For what Melissa calls "bouquet work," nothing compares with these local blooms. "Because Peterkort's stems are thinner than (those of) imported roses, they're very easy to use in hand-tied bouquets. You can group a bunch together for really stunning impact without making the stem too bulky for a bride to handle. And because they are so pliable, the heads don't snap off like thicker, woodier rose stems. I like curving the stems of a Peterkort rose so the bouquet flowers are facing outward rather than up at the bride."

## Meet the rose farmer

Peterkort sells direct to wedding, event and floral designers through its stall at the Portland Flower Market, a five-day-a-week wholesale market owned by the Oregon Flower Growers Association. Here's where you'll find Sandra early in the mornings, personally filling orders, consulting with designers, and serving as the "face" of Peterkort Roses. She's even perky at 6 a.m. "We've always maintained that direct-to-the-florist relationship," she says. "If you have a problem with your product, wouldn't it be nice to talk with the person who actually grew it versus an anonymous grower in South America?"

Being the go-to rose source is nothing new. Peterkort Roses was one of the founding members of the market, which began in 1942 and is now located in Portland's Swan Island Industrial Park. "We get great feedback from designers about rose colors, shapes and ways they are using each variety," Sandra points out. "And we come to the rescue whenever there's a 'floral emergency,' which inevitably occurs on Fridays. We're there for the people who forget to order ahead of time, or who have a last-minute event."

The reciprocal relationship allows Peterkort to share a high level of product information with floral designers. "And in turn, this knowledge allows the designers to tell their customers the story of our roses and how to care for them," Sandra adds.

Sandra, Norman, and their crew of 15 employees are indeed the last rose growers in Oregon. A message on the company's web site helps to explain their popularity: "What can we say about a bunch of people who are still dedicated to growing cut flower roses in the U.S.? Though most of our former colleagues have been knocked out, we continue because we are obsessed."

**Above, from top:** Peterkort's roses blend beautifully with other fresh ingredients to create mixed floral arrangements; a clutch of free-range hens (plus one bossy rooster) reside in Peterkort's greenhouses where they happily feast on weeds and pests that would otherwise diminish the floral crops.

## How to grow a sustainable rose

Commitment and creativity are essential tools to maintain intensive, year-round rose production in Peterkort's 16 greenhouses in Hillsboro, Oregon, which falls in U.S. Department of Agriculture's Zone 8 (minimum winter temperatures of 10-20 degrees Fahrenheit).

"In some ways, we've come full circle," Norman says. "In the old days, when our grandparents were growing roses, they were doing it organically, such as spreading cow manure to fertilize." Today, the company uses as many sustainable growing practices as possible. "Roses do require extra care," he acknowledges, "with a lot of direct human intervention to keep them healthy and productive." Here are some of the practices in place:

- During the winter months, Peterkort increases the amount of artificial light used in the greenhouses, thereby producing more flowers in less space with the same amount of heat.

- Energy curtains have been installed in each greenhouse for added insulation. Made of Mylar and suspended from wires along the greenhouse roof, the panels are closed at night, containing the heat within.

- Working with the Oregon State University Extension Service, Peterkort has developed its own Integrated Pest Management (IPM) approach. The insect ecosystem uses biological controls to suppress aphids, spider mites, thrips and white flies, predators who favor roses.

- Diseases are suppressed by controlling the growing environment, including maintaining ideal temperature, humidity and air circulation levels. Peterkort selects disease-resistant rose varieties and keeps the growing area cleared of dead leaves and debris. "Sometimes, though, the outside conditions are just too overwhelming and we must spray to save the roses," Sandra says. "We use mild solutions that the Environmental Protection Agency designates 'reduced risk,' which are safer to handle, do not require protective clothing or restricted re-entry times."

- A clutch of resident chickens and one rooster not only live inside the greenhouses, they help with weed and pest control. Left to "freely range," the hens can be found pecking at tasty bugs and weeds in between the flower rows.

- All packaging is recycled and roses are wrapped for market in newspaper purchased from a local charity.

# MAIL-ORDER ORGANIC

**A Chico, California, flower farm takes on the gigantic 1-800 florist industry, offering bouquet-givers and their recipients an enticing alternative – organic blooms harvested and shipped the same day**

There's a gorgeous spot on the map, located about 90 miles north of the state capital in a valley between the Sierra Nevada mountain range and the Sacramento River. It's home to a vibrant agricultural community where all sorts of farming operations – almonds, rice, kiwi, olives, peaches and plums – grow on this region's fertile land.

On one of these farms, rows and rows of uncommonly beautiful flowers grow in fields where only organic practices are used. Here's where **Marc Kessler** and **Julia Keener**, a talented and entrepreneurial couple, and their team of "farm girls," an all-female crew, operate as California Organic Flowers, based in Chico. They grow 100-percent-organic blooms, create gorgeous bouquets and ship their just-picked designs all over the country. With a passion for the natural, seasonal beauty of each flower, and blessed with a benign farming climate, they grow floral crops during each month of the year, satisfying the demand from eager mail-order customers and loyal fans who shop at Chico's two farmers' markets.

## A day on the farm

Marc and Julia hesitated when we floated the idea of letting a photographer and writer shadow their operation during the week leading up to Mother's Day – California Organic Flowers' single biggest selling event on the calendar. In one week, the farm creates and delivers more than 400 bouquets coast-to-coast. They could probably ship more flowers, but Mother's Day orders practically clean out the fields, down to every last peony stem.

We promised to stay out of the way and be unobtrusive. While David explored ways to visually capture the magic of their story, I tried my hand with the crew. Julia taught me the right way to strip and clean off foliage from the stems of dianthus, lilies, snapdragons and other flowers.

(Hint: Pull downward on the leaves to remove them from the stems; only the topmost 6 to 8 inches of stem should have foliage.) This essential task occurs while standing at long tables under an open-air shade structure next to the growing fields. We processed those blooms only moments after they were harvested.

After each flower variety is prepped and bunched, the blooms are placed in buckets of water and carted via wagons to the bouquet-making operation in Marc and Julia's garage on the opposite side of the street. A former three-car garage is now home to a walk-in cooler in one bay and efficient assembly and shipping stations in the rest of the space. It's important to harvest flowers during the cooler morning hours. By noon, the crew takes a lunch break, after which they begin making bouquets and filling shipping orders.

Working swiftly and confidently, crew members Lisa Kieren and Mari Piazzisi bundle dozens and dozens of "Happy Mother's Day" bouquets, each of which contains four gorgeous red lilies called 'Black Out' (each flower stem bears 4 or 5 plump buds), 10 white or yellow snapdragons and a collar of magenta pink Sweet Williams (also called dianthus).

All this for as little as $45? "We want people to think it's the best bouquet they

**Above, from top:** An early-morning harvest finds Julia Keener, co-founder with her husband Marc Kessler of California Organic Flowers, collecting gorgeous, rosy-pink stalks of *Watsonia,* a fragrant gladiola relative; indigo-blue irises and clusters of peach lilies are bunched and ready for the market.

**Opposite:** Marc Kessler works with Lisa Kieren, the farm's chief bouquet-maker, to package and ship hundreds of beautiful peony stems. Every peony that's ready to pick is harvested to meet the demand of Mother's Day orders.

ever received," Marc explains, throwing his arms wide to make his point. When recipients open up the box of blooms (packaged in a 100% post-consumer recycled cardboard), they read the message: "California Grown, Solar Powered, Recycled Materials, Family Farmers."

Marc contends that a box of his farm's organically-grown blooms can go head-to-head with conventional mail-order flowers and come out on top. "If you ordered a $50 bouquet from us or any other online source, you'd look at an equal value of flowers. But unlike a dozen roses, the mixed bouquets we send have a lot of stems. I tell my packers to put in as many flowers as the box will hold."

Yes, the flowers are shipped overnight via Federal Express, and Marc often has to address the obvious question about the "carbon footprint" of that exercise. "Most mail-order flowers and roses delivered by the local florist come from farms in South America – three times the distance that we ship flowers from Chico to New York City, for example. There is an environmental cost even with our method and I think if people can find locally-grown flowers in their area, it's the first best thing they should do. But we fill a role of providing flowers to places that may not have year-round access to locally-grown flowers or prepared bouquets."

## From their farm to your vase

Marc and Julia used to live on the Idaho side of the Tetons where they ran a small food-growing operation, enduring what Julia describes as the "shortest growing season in the nation." In the winter of 1995, they visited Chico to explore the options for farming in a gentler climate. "We met great people; we were welcomed," Julia explains, linking her arm in Marc's and smiling. "We kept coming back to work during the winters and began to love the lifestyle."

By 2002, the couple made the leap, relocating to a three-acre farm in Chico with their son, Tava. They embraced the lifestyle of a small-town agricultural community, where they committed their farm to growing only flower crops, supplying blooms to wedding and special event customers.

With a reputation for high-quality flowers, their Terra Bella Flower Farm gained the devoted following of local customers who buy bunches and bouquets at the all-year Chico Saturday Farmers' Market and the six-month-a-year Thursday night market in downtown Chico. But in a college town of 100,000, local buyers can only absorb so much floral capacity; Marc and Julia were convinced they could serve a broader customer base – people hungry for flowers grown organically on a family farm, rather than mass produced and imported.

In 2005, they changed the farm's name and launched California Organic Flowers. You could call it the "anti-FTD." Their online flower shop is built on a different business model, one that may not generate the sales volume of their giant competitors, but instead operates on a values-based system of sustainable practices and individual service.

Marc has invested considerable time and money in R&D to differentiate COF's online bouquet business from all the mass-market and non-organic flower competitors. He tests the farm's cut flowers in the most difficult situations to see how they perform. "I've left a box of flowers out in the sun for 48 hours and then opened it up and put the flowers in a vase to see how they do," he says. The result? Surprisingly great. Now, Marc gives every new variety this rigorous 48-hour test before offering it for sale online. For orders that include a glass vase, Marc actually tests how the contents of a shipping box withstand a several foot high drop to make sure the packaging is durable enough to protect the contents. (And don't think these scenarios are unusual. Marc has heard and seen it all!)

The corporate philosophy of California Organic Flowers, as outlined on its web site, is a soulful one:

**Above:** Julia and Mari transport buckets of just-picked blooms by wagon. Their destination is the bouquet-making station across the street from the flower fields.

## The Beauty of Organic Flowers

It's this simple: Flowers bring the joy and beauty of nature into your home. If there is a sad story of chemical sprays and exploited workers behind your flowers, the joy of the flowers is diminished.

Yes, there are many other great reasons to choose organic – less dangerous chemicals in the environment, more farm acreage managed in a way that builds and enriches valuable soils, and conservation of water. But for us it's more than all that scientific rational stuff, it's a celebration of everything beautiful, natural, and healthy. Flowers are our way of celebrating nature, and celebrating ourselves, so they just have to be grown in a way that cares for the environment or it defeats their whole purpose.

## Organic Pricing

The widespread assumption that anything organically-grown costs more at the cash register is one that farmers of edible crops have faced for years. And now that organic labeling has become a marketing and sales device for packaged food products, it's difficult to analyze how organic practices factor into potato chips or peanut butter that's labeled organic.

Against this backdrop, Marc and Julia's commitment to organic flower farming is both their personal philosophy and smart business. "Using organic practices is the best way to farm," Marc says. "I've really never believed that if organic is what it purports to be, it should cost the consumer more."

**Above, from top:** *Dianthus* is known for its lovely sweet fragrance and long vase life. The farm grows many different colors of this crop, including an enticing fuchsia-pink variety; the farm is proud to add the CCOF labeling to bouquets and bunches, designating its California Certified Organic Farmers status.

**Opposite:** Beneficial insects abound at California Organic Flowers, an indication that Marc and Julia maintain a harmonious, natural balance in their fields.

He points out that organic flower farmers enrich the soil by planting cover crops rather than dosing it with synthetic fertilizers and pesticides. For example, Marc says one 50-pound bag of legume seeds used to grow a cover crop will provide the *same* fertilization as 1,000 pounds of 8-percent nitrogen fertilizer.

"We do not charge more for our organically-grown flowers because we believe that if organic farming is going to be successful in the long run, it needs to prove itself economically. It has been our experience that organic farming is more efficient than conventional farming and as such, should be able to compete on price."

California Organic Flowers doesn't rely on its mail-order business alone, although shipping fresh flowers around the country throughout the year accounts for about 50 percent of the farm's revenue. The balance comes from direct sales to local farmers' market customers.

"We sell everything for $5 per bunch," Marc says. When I express my surprise at this incredibly low price, he laughs and says: "When we came to the market, we had to drive the price up to $5 at the time – the other flower-sellers were only charging $3 per bunch."

This quantity-to-value-to-cost equation makes sense, once you listen to Marc's rationale. First, selling at the farmers' market gives California Organic Flowers a steady cash flow each week. And when you sell to 400 to 500 customers each week, that adds up quickly.

"While other flower stands might be staffed with two to three people, we keep our costs down because we only staff with one person, and making change for $5 bunches is easy." Second, the weekly market gives COF a reliable way to sell excess crops quickly.

"We sell mixed bunches and single varieties. If a customer wants an arrangement with ornamental peppers and sunflowers, they spend $10 for two bunches and combine them."

Selling locally, on a face-to-face basis, also allows Marc and Julia to educate their customers about the care they take to grow, harvest and process each floral variety. "At the farm, each one of our crops has its own page of detailed instructions of when it should be picked, how it should be picked, what happens after it's picked," Marc says. "Julia is always out there showing our harvesters how to gently squeeze the neck of every zinnia bloom before they pick it to make sure it's at the right stage. So our customers have learned that our flowers will last longer because of our practices."

The flowers also bring delight to those who swap a $5 bill for a bouquet of up to 20 stems. "We've trained our customers to expect something unique and fun," he says. "We try to include a 'wow' element in every bouquet. People love smelling a tuberose for the first time or discovering that ornamental peppers or hibiscus pods are gorgeous floral ingredients."

Indeed, on this modest patch of only three acres there is a compelling balance between flower-farming economics and one family's eco-values. And the consumers who enjoy bouquets from this farm reap the benefits.

## The ABCs of Organic Flower Farming

Here are some of the practices that have earned California Organic Flowers its certified organic status from the California Certified Organic Farmers (CCOF), an organization that certifies to the USDA National Organics Program:

**Field preparation:** Organic practices start with healthy soil. "Healthy plants will resist insects and viruses, in the same way a healthy person will fend off sickness and disease," Marc says.

**Fertilizer:** Organic fertility programs provide moderate, sustained nutrition to plants. "Chemical fertilizers are the 'white sugar' of the fertilizer world," he explains. "They provide a quick and unhealthy burst of nutrition that leaves plants susceptible to diseases and pests. Chemical fertilizers are not allowed to be used on certified organic farms."

**Pest and Disease control:** Ideally, says Marc, pests and diseases are controlled on an organic farm by maintaining healthy soil and plant life, and by encouraging a balanced farm ecosystem prolific with populations of predatory microbes, insects and birds. "We have huge resident populations of ladybugs, green lace wings and dragonflies on our farm and we maintain bluebird and barn owl boxes. When an organic farm is in balance, little or no additional application of even approved organic biological or botanical pesticides are required."

**Irrigation:** California Organic Flowers has minimized its water use by installing drip irrigation.

**Cover Crops:** This organic agricultural method is the best way to build soil health and soil fertility on an organic farm. Between each floral crop's "season," Marc and Julia plant nutrient-rich crops such as vetch, peas and other legumes, which add nitrogen to the soil, suppress weeds and create a rich habitat for beneficial insects. The cover crops grow all winter long and are mowed down and worked into the field in the spring. Marc likens this practice to "feeding vitamins to your soil."

# ROCKY MOUNTAIN FLOWERS

## Vibrant, Colorado-grown flowers tell a story of one farming family – and their stewardship of the land

The Boulder County Farmers' Market opens for the season on the first Saturday in April and continues through the third Saturday in November. Reputed to be the state's only exclusively grower-served public market, the 25-year-old farmer-run enterprise is where buyers from all around the Boulder-Denver region can find luscious-looking (and tasting) produce, freshly-bottled honey, artisanal baked goods and locally-grown plants and flowers.

We arrived early one May morning to meet **Chet and Kristy Anderson** of The Fresh Herb Company. The Andersons had attended our lecture at the Denver Botanic Gardens earlier in the week, but we were eager to see in person how this talented couple grows and sells flowers, Rocky Mountain style. Even though they live in USDA Zone 5 (-10 to -15 degrees Fahrenheit average minimum temperatures), which means little farming occurs from November to April, the Andersons have built their farm into a thriving family business.

If our visit to the farmers' market was any indication, the success of The Fresh Herb Company demonstrates that locally-grown flowers can give a farm its competitive edge. This cultural shift in the way people respond to high-quality blooms is due in no small part to passionate individuals like Chet and Kristy and their commitment to sustainable farming.

Belle Anderson, Chet's vivacious mother, greeted us with a generous smile and obvious pride in her offspring's enterprise. She's been handling sales at The Fresh Herb Company's stall from day one, when in 1987, Chet and a half dozen other growers established the market. While Kristy and Belle readied for the day's opening, Chet took David and me on a tour. As we tasted delicious samples of fruit and admired the cornucopia of produce-laden tables, it was apparent to us that Chet is the unofficial mayor of the market. He has a ready "Hello, how's it going?" and a warm handshake for everyone he meets, from longtime friends and fellow vendors to regular shoppers. This is a fabulous community of like-minded individuals who come together for the simple transactions between farmer and customer.

Since it was still early in the season, The Fresh Herb Company's stall was stocked with lots of 11-inch hanging baskets overflowing with a cheery mix of annuals, just in time for Mother's Day gift-giving. Racks of culinary herbs in 4-inch pots enticed foodies eager to get their kitchen gardens planted. And taking center stage: hundreds of long-stemmed Asiatic and Oriental lilies.

Thanks to the bright, warm environment inside The Fresh Herb Company's 15,000-square-foot greenhouse, these lilies are the first cut flower crops of the season. "We could grow a lot more in the greenhouse if we had more space," Chet says. "But for now, our scale and market size are pretty well aligned, allowing us to concentrate on the quality of our plants and flowers and the value they bring to customers."

## Farm Visit

Next, we accompanied Chet to the 10-acre family farm in Longmont, about 20 minutes from Boulder, where he and Kristy had agreed to host a group from the Denver Botanic Gardens on a farm tour – a follow-on to our talks earlier that week. We gladly tagged along, camera and notebook in hand, to watch and record yet another facet of The Fresh Herb Company's unfolding story.

Chet and Kristy meld their sustainable farming philosophy with smart business practices. They serve as a model for newer flower farmers who wish to generate a living wage from their land. Like many contemporary farmers, theirs is a lifestyle pursued with intentionality, Chet says. A native of Boulder, he was close to completing a Master's in Urban Planning when he discovered the writings of poet and essayist Wendell Berry. Smitten with the notion of stewarding and preserving his own corner of the earth, Chet realized that "I wanted to be a farmer rather than fly a desk."

**Top:** Inside 15,000-square-feet of greenhouses, The Fresh Herb Company gets a jump on springtime, planting hundreds of hanging baskets, culinary herbs and lilies for the cut flower trade.

**Opposite:** Flower farmer Chet Anderson, pictured at the Boulder County Farmers' Market, has been growing cut flowers for nearly 25 years. He and his wife Kristy Anderson have expanded The Fresh Herb Company to a successful operation that supplies 30 Whole Foods grocery outlets in five states.

Avid foodies, Chet and Kristy started The Fresh Herb Company in 1983, growing culinary herbs, baby vegetables and salad greens for high-end restaurants in Boulder and Denver.

"Even when we specialized in herbs and salad greens, we always grew flowers to sell at the Boulder County Farmers' Market," Chet points out. When organic salad mixes crossed the line from field crops to processed food, they divested that arm of the business to focus only on culinary herbs, hanging baskets and cut flowers, including perennials, annuals and blooms from flowering shrubs.

Hugging the curve of the bucolic, tree-lined Lefthand Creek, six of the farm's 10 acres are planted with cut flower crops. The property contains highly desirable loamy soil – "You can grow just about anything in this dirt," Chet maintains. The seeds of annual larkspur, bachelor's buttons, bells of Ireland and corn cockle are direct-sown in fields irrigated by pond water that's pumped through a series of natural sand filters and over-head irrigation lines. Perennials, including monk's hood, Jerusalem sage, phlox, Veronica and peonies, reliably produce blooms year after year. Even during Colorado's hot summers, the climate here is moderated by cool air that settles by the creek every evening. Pests and diseases are nearly non-existent, thanks to proper selection of disease-resistant varieties and sustainable cultural practices that encourage the beneficial insects that feed on pests. Inside the greenhouse, rows of luscious lilies grow near tables of herb seedlings. Hundreds of seasonal hanging baskets create a verdant canopy overhead – all are given their early-spring start inside the sheltered setting. Chet and Kristy also lease an 18-acre parcel down the road, where they grow numerous varieties of sunflowers, zinnias and ornamental grasses to sell for cut bunches and bouquets. It's their own little slice of Provence in Colorado!

Farm visits are welcome, giving the gregarious Chet a storytelling platform. "Everybody has one reason or another for buying local, be it shrinking your carbon footprint or employing local youth. But ultimately, people are drawn to our plants and flowers by the story they tell: that they are grown by friends down the street who live in the old schoolhouse; that they are beautiful, fresh-picked and will last in a vase for days and days."

## Farm to Customer

Today, among other outlets, The Fresh Herb Company sells herbs, planted baskets, flowers and bouquets to 30 Whole Foods stores in Colorado, New Mexico, Utah,

Missouri and Kansas. "Whole Foods does a great job of telling the story of the farmers they support," Chet says. He credits the success of the farmer-market relationship to Whole Foods' outstanding commitment to local growers and his own pledge to provide the retail chain with superior products.

Chet and Kristy take care to nurture their Whole Foods relationship. "We're very accessible," Chet says. "We have groups of Whole Foods people out here during the summer for lunches and tours – from the accountants to the regional produce people to staff of individual stores. Coming here helps them better tell our story to their customers."

According to Robert Glover, the produce and floral coordinator for Whole Foods' Rocky Mountain Region, the company defines "locally-sourced" as product grown within a seven-hour radius by truck. Many of the stores in his five-state region also carry "micro-local" produce that may be grown within a two-hour radius. "We really want to see seasonal, local, organic and good value," Glover says. "When they all hit together, that's beautiful."

Whole Foods shoppers have a high awareness and often a personal connection with locally-grown products. So when The Fresh Herb Company's flowers are labeled "Grown in Colorado," it resonates. "We at Whole Foods love being able to work with a grower like Chet, especially because we're able to meet face-to-face, visit his farm and invite him into our stores," Glover says. "It's hard to even think about putting a price on that relationship – it's such an intangible."

The Fresh Herb Company's high-quality flowers are also in demand elsewhere in the Rocky Mountain region. "A lot of flower consumption is happening at the supermarket level," Chet says. "As the availability of fresh, locally-produced, specialty cut flowers increases, we'll see more and more participation from independent retailers and floral designers. But we're just scratching the surface of the opportunity to get our product to these end users."

**Above:** A medley of mixed annuals spills over the edge of a hanging basket, one of 5,000 baskets that The Fresh Herb Company plants and sells each spring.

## A Year on a Flower Farm, by the Numbers

"Our bouquets are always something non-formulaic," Chet says. "We use complementary or contrasting colors; a combination of greenery and woody textures; and varied heights of stems."

12,000 mixed bouquets

25,000 sunflower bunches

10,000 lily bunches

10,000 peony bunches

5,000 hanging baskets

100,000 potted herbs

# Flower Patch Politics

## Driven by tenacity and passion, organic flower farmer Tara Kolla has thrived, despite many odds, in the heart of Los Angeles

In 2003, **Tara Kolla** left a career in public relations and marketing to grow romantic rows of sweet peas in her half-acre Los Angeles backyard and sell them by the bunch at her local farmers' market. In doing so, she never expected to become the poster child of the city's urban farming movement.

**Above:** When Los Angeles flower farmer Tara Kolla was forced to take a hiatus from growing ornamental flowers, she diversified into edible crops, such as cilantro, arugula, basil and other microgreens.

**Opposite:** In addition to her own small backyard, Tara now uses donated land to grow fields of cut flowers for market. In the foreground, her late-season zinnias explode with color.

But that's exactly what happened six years later when disgruntled neighbors turned her in to L.A.'s Department of Building and Safety for selling her flowers at market. Claiming it was inappropriate for her to use residential land for farming, composting and teaching occasional organic gardening classes, several residents on her street effectively shut down Silver Lake Farms, Tara's small, commercial cut flower business, in the middle of her 2009 season.

It turns out that since 1946, the city had defined residential "truck gardening" as only the cultivation of *vegetables* for off-site sale. "I don't know why my neighbors don't like what I do," she says. "I hired a mediator to figure out what the problem was, but unfortunately, that didn't help – nor did my gifts of flower arrangements. They were just being spiteful. My flowers didn't hurt or harm them in any way, since I wasn't selling flowers here…I was selling them at the farmers' market." After city officials ordered Tara to cease marketing her sweet peas and other blooms, "all I could do was give my flowers away and ask for donations."

Facing fines, jail time or a costly legal battle to obtain a land-use variance, Tara dug in her heels and decided to lobby for a change to the ordinance. "I didn't want to lose, give in or submit," she says. Tara's fierce belief in justice helped sustain her during a yearlong fight for what became known as the Food & Flowers Freedom Act, although she acknowledges that it took a toll on her physically, emotionally and financially.

Yet Tara feels grateful for the wave of support from her community, including long-time Silver Lake Farmers' Market customers and fellow urban farming activists. "So many people worked so hard to help me, writing letters and coming to hearings," Tara says. Her confident British accent and striking appearance, not to mention her savvy public relations skills, attracted media attention and thrust Tara into the role as spokes-person for everything from sustainable agriculture to the plight of the small family farm.

Above and opposite, top: Claire Acosta, Tara's only full-time employee, harvests microgreens. These are now just one of Silver Lake Farms' multiple channels of business.

"This ordinance helps increase access to locally-grown flowers and healthy, fresh foods and sets clear rules to avoid confusion between neighbors and the city," says L.A. City Council President Eric Garcetti. "This is a big step forward for urban farming here in Los Angeles that can be a model for other cities across the nation."

## Home grown again

During her furlough from flowers Tara reinvented and diversified Silver Lake Farms. "I had to do something while waiting for the law to change." She organized a Community-Supported Agriculture (CSA) service with a local farmer and began growing microgreens like arugula, cilantro and basil where the sweet peas and ranunculus blooms previously flourished. She planted a huge crop of natural loofah, which is technically a vegetable (since it is a pumpkin relative) that when dried is sold as a body-care sponge. And she launched an organic garden care service, attracting customers from all around Los Angeles.

At one important L.A. Planning Commission hearing in March 2010, thirty attended to support Tara's position, while only a single opponent, one of the neighbors, appeared. When the commission unanimously voted to endorse the proposed truck gardening changes, Tara finally felt as if the end was in sight. "I thought, 'wow, this is really going to pass,'" she says, with emotion in her voice.

On May 21, 2010, the Los Angeles City Council unanimously approved changes to the truck gardening ordinance, permitting owners of residential properties to cultivate and sell flowers. An amended city code now means that Angelinos have greater access not just to locally-grown vegetables, but also to flowers, nuts, herbs and fruits in every season.

But Tara didn't give up on her original passion. On the day the truck gardening law passed, she broke ground at a new flower patch – a 6,000-square-foot piece of vacant land donated to Silver Lake Farms by friends of some of Tara's landscaping clients. It was Tara's to use without the threat of legal action. "A whole gang came to support me and help me get the rows and trenches prepped for planting," she recalls. The growing ground is located

in Glassell Park, a neighborhood about a mile from Tara's home, but the Silver Lake Farms crew nicknamed it "Groovy Canyon" for its hilly terrain. The property owners now enjoy attractive rows of zinnias, sunflowers, rudbeckias, cleomes and anemones. But to achieve this abundance took 75 yards of compost donated by Eric Wilhite from Community Recycling, a lot of sweat equity, and several pickaxes to prep the soil before Tara's seedlings could be planted.

She can't exactly clone herself, but the new truck gardening law does allow Tara to employ one person at her home-based business. She often works side-by-side with her assistant Claire Acosta, a recent graduate of University of California at Santa Cruz's ecological horticulture program. They tend to trays of microgreens, although Tara planned to reinstall dozens of frames for her signature bloom: pink, purple, white and red sweet peas for the season ahead. The secret to success with sweet peas, she points out, "is to keep cutting the flowers so the vines produce more and more." One sniff of the heady, romantic fragrance and it's no surprise why these are her favorite flowers of all.

Another employee works one to two days per week at Groovy Canyon, and of course Tara still logs time caring for several clients' vegetable gardens. But now that she is able to refocus her flower farming efforts, she wonders how she can juggle everything. "I had no idea that what I chose to do while waiting to sell flowers again would take off," she admits, breaking into a grin as she tours us through the new flower patch where irresistible zinnias in carnival colors line the paths. "I have a lot on my plate, but it's good and I'm fortunate."

Yes, she is a poster child for flower farming. But now, rather than spending hours lobbying city hall, Tara can be found at some of the most popular neighborhood markets in Los Angeles, selling bountiful bunches of fresh, organic, local flowers to customers old and new.

Her passion for flowers isn't one Tara often puts to words, but when asked to, she tells this story: "A funny little man with a red nose and knitted skull cap summed it up for me one day as he was passing my flower stand. You see, I've never been able to quite put my finger on what it is that makes naturally-grown, sun-kissed flowers glow and sparkle the way they do. They just seem to draw people in — at least, people open to that kind of natural, sweet beauty," she says. "He looked at me and said, *'There are fairies about your flowers.'* I think he might have been an elf."

**Above:** Tara began her flower farm raising enchanting sweet peas, and after a publicized struggle she recently won the right to grow and market them again. Silver Lake Farms grows custom sweet pea mixes from Renee's Seeds and named English varieties. "I start the season with 'Winter Elegance'; then I move to Royals, then gradually I move to the Spencer types," Tara says. "I love Spencers. 'Blue Danube' is my favorite."

# Grower Wisdom

**Above:** A native of Santiago, Chile, Joan Thorndike now grows cut flowers for weddings and flower shops in Oregon's agriculturally-rich Rogue River Valley.

**Opposite:** During the peak of peony season in May and June, Joan harvests peonies once in the morning and once in the evening, during cooler hours of the day.

## Early Adopter

Growing flowers organically for 20 years, Le Mera Gardens has changed its community, one locally-grown bouquet at a time.

Flower farmer **Joan Thorndike** raises more than 100 types of certified organic fresh-cut flowers, varieties that are breathtakingly beautiful, high in quality and guaranteed to exceed the expectations of the florists and brides and grooms who order from her farm. When it's delivery day, she receives an ecstatic welcome, due both to the sheer diversity of stems and blooms, and the sensory pleasure that people experience when they smell, touch and hold her just-harvested botanicals.

Joan's Le Mera Gardens supplies florists, weddings, special events, homes, charities and restaurant accounts in Medford, Ashland, and several other southern Oregon and northern California cities. Lately, she has had bridal parties come to her from as far away as Portland, 325 miles to the north.

"They might find me on the Internet, but word-of-mouth is the number one way brides hear about me," she says. These are self-selected clients, those for whom seasonal, farm-grown flowers are a priority. They may assemble their own bouquets

and centerpieces or ask a florist to design with Le Mera's blooms. Whether they spend $100 or $3,000 for wedding flowers, each will be unique, Joan says. "There are brides who want something very seasonal and simple and others who have a specific palette or complex design in mind – and yet they're all beautiful."

Joan's friendly, confident attitude is just what an anxious bride or mother-of-the bride needs to hear over the phone, which is usually how the first contact occurs. She does a lot of virtual hand-holding, especially when explaining Le Mera's system: Wedding clients come to her farm on the Tuesday morning before the nuptials to "shop" for their blooms from her well-stocked refrigerated flower truck. "I know this sounds scary but it will work," she assures them.

Upon hearing of this method, nervous wedding parties are encouraged to visit one of several Rogue River Valley area farmers' markets where Fry Family Farm, Le Mera's farming partners, sells from the same fields that produce Joan's crops. If still unconvinced, they can also walk through the growing fields, "to see that our flowers are beautiful, vibrant and fresh," Joan says. Further assurances can be found on her web site, which has a week-by-week availability calendar so brides can project in advance what's in bloom near the day of the wedding. "With 10 acres, there's plenty of variety. We live in a very generous growing area."

When the bride arrives at Le Mera Gardens, she peruses the "visual candy" displayed on racks inside Le Mera's shop-on-wheels. During summer and early fall there may be four consultations each week. Joan talks with clients about budget, flower options and color palette, agreeing on the weekend's order.

The flowers are harvested on Wednesday, professionally hydrated overnight and stored in Le Mera's barn for Thursday pickup. Joan's favorite part is receiving photographs after the big day, as she never ceases to be surprised by the many ways flower choices reflect the bride's individual personality and style.

## Grower's Wisdom: Peonies

The peony (Paeonia lactiflora) – with its plump, multi-petaled perfection in a romantic color spectrum ranging from creamy white to blood red – is a fashionable flower for bridal bouquets. But the harvest season for this herbaceous perennial, which grows from a rhizomatous tuber, is relatively short – from four to six weeks, depending on the region. For Joan Thorndike, who harvests blooms from several hundred double peony plants each year, this means she can sell every peony stem she cuts in May and June. Here is some of her grower's wisdom:

- **When to harvest:** Cut them "in bud" for maximum vase life. Gently squeeze the bud. If it's squishy like a marshmallow, with an easy give, the time is right.

- **How to postpone the bud's opening:** Use Joan's "dry-storage" method. Cut the flowers at their "marshmallow" stage and bundle. Store flat, in a cooler or the crisper drawer of a refrigerator. The flowers can be saved at this stage for up to one month. A day or two prior to your wedding or event, "re-cut the stems, put them in a vase and they'll burst open so they're perfect."

**Above:** A flowering bulb expert, Jan Roozen is eager to meet and talk with his customers. "For me, it's more than just a business," he explains. "It is really important that the person who enjoys the flowers I grow does so for a week or even 10 days."

**Opposite:** Jan suggests that you keep daffodil stems separate from other flowers, such as inside a water-filled plastic bag, to ensure long-lasting mixed arrangements. Or, for the best results, display daffodils in their own vase of water.

## Dutch Master

Jan Roozen brings old-world experience to a modern, market-driven industry by growing gorgeous cut flowers for florists and bulbs for fellow farmers.

**Jan Roozen** has one foot in the past and another in the 21st century. His is the 8th generation of Roozens to grow flowering bulbs and Jan can trace his family's profession to the 16th century.

Covering six acres in Washington's Skagit Valley, Choice Bulb Co. is one of those places that cause near-fender-benders during bloom season. Parking tickets on Beaver Marsh Road are not uncommon, as people stop to photograph fields of iconic spring daffodils and tulips or lesser-known foxtail lilies and ornamental alliums. Bulbs, especially viewed *en masse* in tidy agricultural rows, can be mesmerizing. Taking them home to display in a vase is a seasonal ritual signaling the arrival of spring. One never tires of it.

As a young man, Jan left Heemstede, Holland, and migrated to North America, eventually settling in Washington State's Skagit Valley to join a bulb-farming uncle.

Eleven years later, in 1982, Jan's independent streak won out when he and the uncle parted ways. Nearly 40, Jan and his wife Ritva started Choice Bulb Co. with a small inventory of bulbs. "We had nothing to fall back on and my knowledge was the only security I had," he recalls. "But my wife said, 'You have nothing to lose.' And you know, we did better that first year than all those years when I worked for my uncle."

The Roozens own some of the land they farm and lease the rest, a smart strategy motivated by their belief that fields should be rotated and planted with cover crops between seasons, practices that not only prevent diseases, but also help keep varieties intact and growing fields tidy.

One of Jan's bestsellers is the foxtail lily *(Eremurus* x *issabellinus)*, a hybrid of the six-foot-high or taller spire with Central Asian origins. Foxtail lilies leave Jan's farm in boxes of 50, which cost $3 per stem wholesale. By the time a floral designer halfway across the country purchases the buttercream-yellow or apricot-hued flower, she expects to spend upwards of $9 per stem. In between, the shipper and the wholesaler take their cut, prices fluctuating with variables like shipping and labor.

The economic downturn and shrinking floral budgets for big corporate events have affected growers of specialty cut flowers, Jan says. He also blames skyrocketing transportation fees and competition from cheap imports for shaking his once-healthy business model. Yet he finds room for optimism: "The one thing that is starting to work in our favor is that as transportation costs keep climbing, we become more competitive than the imported flowers."

While he continues to ship cut flowers and bulbs to customers across the U.S., Jan takes great pleasure in showing up most Sundays to sell flowers at the University District Farmers' Market in Seattle, about 60 miles south of his farm. This is where he dispenses all that flower wisdom, greeting new and repeat customers with his alluring smile and Dutch-accented advice. If the flower world could have its own Sensei, it would be this man.

Growing flowers is not merely a way to make a living, he insists. Like art or music, Jan values flowers for their inherent beauty, which is to him the ultimate reason to grow flowers in the first place. "Some days when I'm out in the fields, doing some farm job, I stop and appreciate the relative quiet around me. I see that the act of growing something – and doing it well – gives me much satisfaction. It shapes my image of myself. Those moments don't happen much, but they are all the more valuable because they aren't all that often."

## Grower's Wisdom: Daffodils

The daffodil, narcissus or jonquil *(Narcissus sp.)* is the harbinger of springtime, with its erect grass-green stems and blades and cheery yellow trumpet-shape blooms. When you meet Jan at the farmers' market, you may be a fortunate recipient of his grower's wisdom about how best to display these plentiful flowers:

• Daffodils have hollow stems that contain a sap-like substance that gives the stem its turgidity. When the flowers are cut, the liquid seeps out, and it can shorten the life of other flowers in the vase. Jan recommends displaying daffodils in a vase by themselves – or, if used within a larger arrangement, keeping the stems separate, in a small, water-filled plastic bag.

## The Flower Lady

Gretchen Hoyt's friendly face is synonymous with her fresh, field-grown blooms, raised with passion and experience.

**Above:** Gretchen Hoyt, of Alm Hill Gardens, and her husband Ben Hoyt, started farming in the mid-1970s. Their year-round fields, greenhouses and high tunnels produce edible crops and flowers. Harvesting lilacs from 70 bloom-laden shrubs is a task that Gretchen attends to.

**Opposite:** Years of experience growing many varieties of fragrant, crowd-pleasing lilacs have taught Gretchen the very best ways to harvest and display these flowers.

**Gretchen Hoyt** describes herself as a back-to-the-land hippy, but now that nearly 40 years have passed, this flower farmer has the kind of lifestyle many urban dwellers dream about. If you view Alm Hill Gardens through rose-tinted glasses, you might think those who live here have a romantic, carefree existence. Yet if you follow Gretchen and her husband **Ben Hoyt** around for a season, you'll instead gain a profound admiration for how their values, sustainable farming practices and sheer hard work produce something so ephemeral and delicate as a lilac, tulip, lily, anemone or peony.

The couple overcame many obstacles to reach this moment: When they planted their first field of raspberries in rural Everson, Washington, just two miles from the Washington-British Columbia border, Gretchen was a single parent of two young children who had escaped from the city. Ben was a veteran of the war in Vietnam who wanted to unplug from society.

"Ben's parents were dairy farmers. I never grew anything until I was 26 years old," Gretchen says. "We had Ben's dad's tractor, no running water and no power, so we started with very little at the beginning." Their efforts grew into one of the first year-round, direct-selling farms in Western Washington. Today, the 47-acre property contains six 30 x100-foot greenhouses, countless high tunnels (hoop houses that can raise temperatures by 10 degrees), and fields of edible crops. And, of course, flowers.

Alm Hill Gardens is known for raising luscious cut tulips, which account for 80 percent of their floral production. At Seattle's Pike Place Market the sign reads: "Alm Hill Gardens: A Small Sustainable Family Farm Since 1974." The stall overflows with irresistible blooms in a vibrant spectrum of hues, to the delight of locals and tourist alike.

Depending on the season, these brilliant gems on plump green stems can sell from $20 to $30 for a bunch of 30. You can find the classic ovoid-shaped tulip, like the orange-and-purple-streaked 'Princess Irene', or more unusual varieties, such as the parrot and French tulips.

## Co-farming to nurture the next generation

Five years ago, after looking for someone to join their farm and potentially take it over, the Hoyts entered into an innovative partnership with Growing Washington, a nonprofit cooperative that shares their sustainable farming philosophy. As a worker-managed venture, Growing Washington is run by a group of younger farmers who grow food to supply neighborhood markets, restaurants, schools, grocery stores and CSAs. The arrangement allows the Hoyts to share their knowledge and experience with the next generation of farmers while also cutting back on the intensive day-to-day farming.

Now focused exclusively on growing flowers, Gretchen and Ben say they have the best of both worlds. If land itself can be autobiographical, indeed Alm Hill tells this couple's story. "I knew I wanted to be a farmer when I finally grew a garden," Gretchen says, smiling. "This is what I was supposed to do." Yes, she has a long mane of snow-white hair, but her youthful energy makes it hard to believe this woman is into her fourth decade as a farmer.

### Grower's Wisdom: Lilacs

Competing with those lovely tulips for a visitor's attention are Alm Hill's lilacs, a springtime sight to behold in dreamy shades of pale to dark violet. Gretchen planted her first lilacs 25 years ago; today, about 70 vigorous shrubs produce from mid-April until Mother's Day. "Lilacs produce flowers on last year's wood, so if you trim them, they'll bounce back and keep producing."

Here are Gretchen's tips for harvesting and prolonging the vase life of your lilacs:

- Harvest lilacs when most of the florets are open, perhaps with a few closed florets at the tip of the bloom. They never open past the stage when you pick them.

- Cut each branch with a stem long enough for arranging. Use sharp, clean pruners.

- Using a sharp knife, "shave" the cut stem as if you are shaving a pencil. This exposes the under bark, which creates more area for water to be absorbed by the flower. A similar method is to slice 1 to 2 inches, and before removing your clippers, make a twist to open up the interior of the stem.

- Lilacs are so beloved because of their fragrance, but the scent begins to wane after they have been cut. Enjoy the moment: This is what seasonality is truly about.

## Heart of the Country

The joy of farming – in every season – sustains the owners of one Oregon flower farm where land, wildlife and people are nurtured.

As farmland matures and evolves, so do those who steward it. Just ask **Charles Little**, who has been tending to ornamental crops in the verdant Willamette Valley since 1986. He describes the 40 abundant acres at the foot of Oregon's Mount Pisgah, where he and his wife **Bethany** grow 250 varieties of fresh flowers, fillers, wildflowers, herbs, ornamental grains and grasses, seasonal berries, pods and branches, as a "horticultural paradise with its own thriving ecosystem."

"I was one of those young men who wanted to create a hippy commune and be a farmer," Charles says of his early years. "I've always wanted to live and make my living on the land." More than 25 years after planting his first flower crops, he maintains that "farming is a lifestyle, a stewardship and commitment to the land and a generous consideration of all life around you, from the beneficial microorganisms and insects, to the birds and snakes."

When starting out, Charles rented 15 acres from a retired peppermint farmer. He planted everlasting crops – annual and perennial flowers that hold their color and form when dried. "I was like a traveling salesman," he recalls of the snapdragons, larkspur, statice and other flowers harvested and delivered to floral and craft wholesalers in Portland.

Today, the flowers harvested from Charles Little & Co.'s fields satisfy demand for nearly every color, form and type of plant ingredient used by wedding, floral and event designers. On the

West Coast, wholesale buyers snap up the prolific farm's field-grown crops at the Los Angeles Flower Market, Portland Flower Market and Seattle Wholesale Growers Market.

## A Growing Passion

During the peak season, from June through October, customers buy direct from Charles and Bethany at their U-Pick flower fields in Eugene, which operate as Sparhawk Farms. Bridal parties consult with Bethany who helps them select their wedding flowers, floral palette and design needs – from full-service bouquets to do-it-yourself. Grower's bunches sell for $6 to $10, and if customers want to harvest their own blooms, the pricing is simple: They pay $4 for as many stems as fit inside a one-inch ring.

There is great value in this approach, Charles says. "Aside from inexpensive access to cut flowers, people who come to our U-Pick fields get to experience farmland under their feet, bask in the northern sun and feel the wind in their faces – just like a flower farmer does every day." Moms and daughters; sisters and cousins; kids, too, visit the farm for flowers. Charles fantasizes about these multigenerational outings: "Can you imagine the bonds that perhaps develop? These bonds – and memories – will be with them forever."

Charles Little & Co. adheres to *permaculture*, or sustainable land-use design. For example, 70 percent of the acreage is occupied by well-established trees, shrubs and herbaceous perennials, plants that "require little care, fertilizer or weeding, and are self-sustaining," Charles explains. "The beauty of plants like ornamental cherry trees or flowering viburnum is that we're doing most of the pruning needed by virtue of doing the harvest. I'm the guy who has the weird shrubbery that's naturalized out in his fields."

Observing the natural cycle of each season is a joyous experience of which he never tires. In fact, Charles describes it as "thrilling to watch when an annual has just enough left over to self-sow, creating a carpet of seedlings in the fall or spring." A little attention, organic fertilizer, the moisture of seasonal showers, and some hand-weeding leads to the anticipation of "the glorious bounty," he adds.

## Grower's Wisdom: Inter-planting

When it comes to land stewardship, Charles relies on both experience and inspiration. He often recalls biodynamic gardening techniques he employed as a young man living at Farallones Institute, a Northern California educational center and commune. "We would inter-plant anything we could think of, like pairing lettuce crops with broccoli crops. By the time the lettuce heads were big and ready to be harvested, we were making space for the long-season cauliflower or broccoli to grow larger."

Here is how this approach is manifested on a flower farm:

**Onions and sweet peas:** "A friend gave us 800 onion sets and we thought, Where are we going to plant these? We'd already planted the sweet peas and I knew the ground was naturally good. So we planted onions on either side of the sweet pea trellis. It ended up being a really great idea because the onions grew and their leaves supported the young sweet peas."

# CHAPTER TWO

# The Eco Designer

*"If flowers aren't locally or organically grown, then they are most likely coming from some huge factory farm. My customers do not want flowers dipped in strong pesticides on their dinner table."*

**– Melissa Feveyear,**
Terra Bella Organic Floral
& Botanical Designs

# THE ACCIDENTAL FLOWER FARMER

**A patch of urban asphalt surrounded by chain link fencing and loops of barbed wire may seem unwelcoming. That is, until you peer inside to discover a designer's bountiful cutting garden in San Francisco's Dog Patch District**

Increasingly, there are designers who, by necessity, harvest floral ingredients from their own gardens. As well, there are growers who assume the role of floral designer, satisfying a bridal customer's request for unique, straight-from-the-farm bouquets. That these two worlds are happily intersecting is due to curiosity, innovation and experimentation on the part of designer and grower alike.

San Francisco-based **Baylor Chapman**, owner of Lila B. Flowers, Gardens and Events, is both designer and flower farmer. She is also a Certified San Francisco Green Business owner who bases her studio philosophy on local and sustainable design practices. Baylor's fashionable, 500-square-foot workshop occupies a loading dock in San Francisco's Mission District, where she and her assistants turn out dazzling, flower-filled vases, bowls and urns. Local and seasonal blooms are used here with abandon. How did all of this come to be?

Early on, Baylor saw that many of her botanical design ideas couldn't be realized because it wasn't always easy to source ingredients locally. For her, the obvious answer was: *"Why not grow those blooms myself?"*

## Urban Farm Scene

She first tried raising flowers on the roof of the warehouse where her street-level studio is housed. The plants took root in soil-filled milk crates lined with screening. "We had to walk up 75 steps to tend to the flowers," Baylor recalls. Stair-climbing wasn't the worst of it, though. All the soil and water had to be hand-carried to the roof just to keep the flowers alive.

It didn't take long for Baylor and her staff to yearn for a ground-level gardening space. "We found an old parking lot about 1½ miles away in a neighborhood called 'Dog Patch' and arranged to rent part of it." Today, the blacktop setting has a thriving crop of city-grown flowers. Perennials, annuals and vines grow in more than 100 recycled 15-gallon nursery pots, the type typically used to grow landscaping trees.

The Lila B. Lot Garden flourishes on this industrial street behind a barbed wire-topped fence. The garden's presence beautifies the neighborhood and has attracted the interest of nearby auto body shop workers who peer admiringly through the chain link when out on their lunch breaks. "Now you see hummingbirds and bees flying around," says the designer, her friendly face breaking into a warm smile. "The car repair guys come out and enjoy it here for lunch. It's sort of a sanctuary."

Her pop-up urban flower farm has helped Baylor gain credibility with clients. Now she can say: "We grew these flowers for you." It allows her to incorporate all sorts of uncommon blooms, berries, foliage and tendrils into her designs and even custom-grow to a bride's specifications.

Among the crops here at Lila B., you'll find salvia, rudbeckia, gaillardia, oat grass, asters, scented geraniums, roses, lamb's ear, sweet peas, veronica, nigella, passionflower,

**Above:** Diminutive botanicals as well as those more dramatic in scale are grown in the Lila B. Lot Garden. Baylor harvested fuzzy lamb's ears foliage, baby-blue forget-me-not blooms and the fruit and leaves of an alpine strawberry to create this sweet boutonniere.

**Opposite:** Undaunted by inner-city conditions that are anything but pastoral, Baylor Chapman runs her design studio from a former loading dock and grows flowers on an asphalt parking lot.

**Previous spread:** Melissa Feveyear (left) owns an organic flower emporium that combines sustainable practices with sophisticated design. She sources fresh and seasonal botanical ingredients from Jello Mold Farm and other local Northwest growers.

sea holly, cosmos, scabiosa, sunflowers, cerinthe and zinnias – as well as plants grown for their fruit and foliage. It is a mind-boggling selection of design ingredients you'd be hard pressed to find in most conventional flower shops. Sophie de Lignerolles, an artist who works for Lila B. as a designer, maintains meticulous spread sheets of the flowers they grow, including varieties grown from seeds and unusual offerings from Annie's Annuals, a specialty and mail-order nursery in the East Bay area, a favorite with the women. "Sophie is propagating from seed now, which I think is pretty fabulous," Baylor says. That means an even greater variety of floral bounty for Lila B.'s customers.

## A Greener Approach

Baylor is well equipped to grow her own unique floral choices, thanks to her landscape design studies. After earning a garden design certificate from University of California at Berkeley Extension, she spent time on the crew of a Bay Area estate garden whose owners valued organic practices and requested that flowers from the grounds would be used for interior bouquets. Baylor soon found herself creating these arrangements. Her interest in floral design lured her into more creative gigs, including freelancing for other studios and shops.

In 2007, Baylor opened Lila B., named after her grandmother. At first, she worked out of the loft where she lives. After one year of literally living with her flowers, she moved her studio across the street to another warehouse. Formerly a commercial laundry, it now houses 60 art studios in an environment that fosters creativity and experimentation. Baylor's tiny workshop was once a warehouse loading dock, so it faces the street and has a huge, roll-up door that brings light and fresh air inside. While not a retail store, the street-front presence wows pedestrians with glimpses of huge arrangements inside – and high above the roll-up door at the front: a trio of frames planted with a living tapestry of succulents.

**Above, from top:** The Lila B. Lot Garden thrives in a rather rugged neighborhood behind a chain-link fence topped with barbed wire. Inside of this fence grows an impressive assortment of botanical ingredients that inspire Baylor's eclectic designs; Baylor and freelance designer Anna Hoffmann (right) prepare a bridal party's personal flowers for an upcoming wedding.

Thanks to Northern California's temperate environment, Baylor enjoys an excellent, almost year-round source of flowers from her suppliers. Besides her own Lila B. home-grown flowers, she takes advantage of San Francisco's wholesale flower market where many California growers bring their crops to sell. A few "weird and wonderful" suppliers are favorites, including two sisters who run a company called Florist at Large. They stock foraged goodies such as fruit, branches and wild ingredients coveted by designers who want a natural look. "I want people to be curious," says Baylor. "I want my bouquets to be beautiful to the eye, but they should also prompt the question: 'What is that? Where does it grow? Can you eat it?'"

We visited Baylor at the peak of summer when she and Anna Hoffmann, a designer who occasionally freelances for her, were creating flowers for a peach-and-ivory-themed wedding – using a combination of tawny 'Cafe au Lait' dahlias, blush-pink garden roses, the silvery foliage of Dusty Miller and lamb's ears, fluffy ornamental grasses, flowering sprigs from a mock orange tree and honeysuckle vines.

As Baylor assembled the groomsmen's boutonnieres with scented geranium foliage and seed heads from the pincushion flowers growing in her Lot Garden, she paused to admire her creation: "Even though flowers are ephemeral, I treat floral design like I do garden design. I think of each arrangement as a mini garden, with its own texture, scale and color palette. They're little masterpieces."

Baylor's bouquets embody both her artistic sensibility and her profound admiration for the plant world's infinite variety of color, form and texture. "I hope that people are drawn to me because of what I'm doing and what I'm interested in doing," she says, "because I feel very blessed."

**Above:** An urban flower farm flourishes as a sensory counterpoint to this gritty industrial neighborhood in San Francisco.

**Below:** Tiny glass bottles are labeled for delivery to the wedding venue. Filled with water, these vessels keep boutonnieres and bouquets fresh until it's time to use them.

## Recycled Style

Baylor prefers using recycled vases, and she values a local salvage yard as one of her secret sources. The workers there "get" what she's doing and enjoy rescuing pieces of scrap copper and silver plate for her. She picks up these salvaged vessels for a song and utilizes them for center-pieces and other arrangements. The aged patina and shapes can look modern or vintage – and complement all sorts of botanical ingredients.

Baylor also repurposes glass light fixtures, turning them into oversized urns. She often rents out (rather than sells) larger containers for special events and weddings, helping keep costs down for brides and party hosts. Clients are encouraged to use vases from their personal cupboards rather than buying something generic for the sake of calling it new.

# THE CUTTING GARDEN

**A floral designer and a nursery owner combine talents to create signature botanical bouquets using local flowers and living plants – with sensational results**

If you've picked up a lifestyle magazine in the past few years, you have probably read about **Flora Grubb**, the brilliant young landscape designer-turned-plant-seller whose eponymous retail nursery in San Francisco is a hotbed of inspiration. In 2007, *House & Garden* magazine named Flora a "garden tastemaker," an accolade which drew national attention to her cutting-edge style of using plants – indoors and outdoors – in a fresh, contemporary way.

In the fall of 2009, Flora introduced flowers to her San Francisco customer base, instantly signaling that a locally-grown (and designed) bouquet was the newest must-have item for style-conscious shoppers. It was customer demand that first motivated Flora Grubb Gardens to add a floral design studio. Wowed by the quirky, natural botanical arrangements used to decorate special events at the garden shop, fans began asking whether the designs were available for purchase.

**Susie Nadler**, whose husband Saul Nadler is Flora's business partner, is the surprise darling of this story. With an MFA in creative writing and a background teaching writing, Susie discovered her love of floral design after initially volunteering to make centerpieces and arrangements for store events. (That's Susie on page 89, holding one of her mixed bouquets.) Without a bit of formal training, she wasn't bound by preconceived rules of design. Instead, she worked with the natural beauty of plants, taking cuttings from some of the nursery's best-selling plants and pairing them with locally-grown cut flowers from vendors at the San Francisco Wholesale Flower Market. Susie quickly garnered a following for her lavish use of foliage, fronds and fruit-laden branches.

It didn't take long for the two women to realize they were incubating a new business concept – one that appealed to Flora Grubb's plant-obsessed core customer base. And so The Cutting Garden came into being, Suzie's floral studio within Flora Grubb Gardens. "Susie has such amazing taste and a very special way of putting flowers and plants together," Flora says. "Her bouquets look like someone has bottled up the store – her flowers and our plants reflect one creative mind."

Susie's style, which evolved as she created wedding bouquets and centerpieces for friends, is clearly influenced by the array of plant material available at her fingertips. Succulents of all kinds may begin as plants in one-gallon nursery pots. But in Susie's design vocabulary they are ingredients that play well with more conventional blooms like dahlias, hydrangeas and garden roses. "The idea that you can have a living plant in your bouquet – one that will live on beyond your wedding day – is appealing to a bride," Susie says of the succulents she uses (see sidebar, page 67). While not dogmatic about it, she naturally gravitates to locally-grown flowers, foliage, stems and petals, many of which trigger memories of her Northern California childhood.

Using plants with memory-evoking textures, fragrances, berries and blooms resonates with brides and grooms whose flower choices are often connected to their ceremony's location, whether under a forest canopy or on a sandy beach. "When I use flowers that remind a bride of how California's hillsides look just after rainy season, for example, I'm helping her capture that special place where the marriage occurs."

This approach also appeals to bridal parties planning a "green wedding" with elements that may range from locally-grown food and flowers to composting and recycling after the reception. At least one-quarter of The Cutting Garden's bridal customers want California-grown flowers in their bouquets for this reason.

San Francisco's hugely popular 'locavore' movement currently encompasses food and wine, art and other lifestyle choices. It's no surprise that "interest in locally-grown flowers is catching up with everything else that's local," Susie says.

**Above:** Flora Grubb curates her San Francisco plant nursery with an eye for design, style and presentation. Displayed among plant groupings are retro-salvaged finds like a bicycle sprouting succulents. This sense of playfulness extends to the work of designer Susie Nadler for The Cutting Garden, the nursery's in-house floral studio.

**Opposite:** Horticultural celebrity Flora Grubb oversees her eponymous urban plant emporium, where palms, succulents, Mediterranean and drought-tolerant plants – and floral design – are the specialties.

When clients learn that many conventionally-grown and imported flowers are produced with great chemical input, it changes the choices they make, Flora adds. "Those flowers on your table are not so pretty anymore."

## Begin With Beautiful

Flora and Susie claim that "neither of us are florists" in the traditional sense of the word. But after launching the floral design studio in time for the 2009 holiday season, which entailed mostly centerpieces and banquet arrangements, the women were inundated with requests for the 2010 wedding season.

They take delight in using the local flora of California, including blooms grown by organic farms in places like Petaluma and Half Moon Bay. "It's easy for Californians to preach *locavorism*," Flora admits. "We could probably survive off of the edible fruit that grows on our street trees here in San Francisco, so we don't have to go across the seas and bring exotic things here."

Yet as one who is often quoted by the media on sustainable landscape design, Flora says she still struggles to find a philosophical balance that makes sense. "You have to ask really thoughtful questions in order to figure out what your heart tells you to consume. Does that mean you buy blueberries from Chile because they are organic? Or do you buy blueberries from a local farm in California that aren't organic but didn't have to travel far to reach you?"

Sometimes we can't appreciate the inherent splendor of a native plant or the charm of a cottage garden perennial, especially when faced with a marketing onslaught that offers us something both exotic and out-of-season. It's not until an artist reinterprets the ordinary as something extraordinary that we see with new eyes. The message may be as simple as transforming a few wild-gathered stems into a stunning floral bouquet. When in doubt, Flora says, "We lead with beautiful. We don't tell people they're here to shop for sustainable garden ideas – all they know is that they just love what they see."

**Above, from top:** Succulents like aeonium (left) and echeveria (right) are transformed into long-stemmed floral ingredients using Susie's method, as outlined in steps 1, 2 and 3 on page 67; seasonal color and texture, in the form of dahlias and Queen Anne's lace, comes from local Bay Area flower farms that supply The Cutting Garden.

## The Succulent Mixed Bouquet

Succulent plants like echeveria, aeonium and graptopetalum – all of which are reminiscent of a flower rosette – are the secret ingredients in Susie Nadler's bouquets and arrangements. Susie likes that these plants often last for months out of the ground (some eventually produce their own roots and can be re-planted to be enjoyed long after a wedding or special event).

"The succulents blend in because of their 'flower' shapes – and they look really great with other cutting garden ingredients."

Follow Susie's techniques to design a bouquet of your own:

**Ingredients for a 12-inch-high vase with a 7-inch opening:**

3-5 floral stems from succulent plants and/or tillandsias

3-5 dahlias and hydrangea blooms in a palette that complements the succulents

6-10 branches of fluffy foliage from a woody shrub (Susie selected *Abelia,* a fragrant shrub with small green leaves and copper-pink sepals.)

6-10 stems of oregano as foliage

A nice mix (6-10 stems each) of accents, including dark purple pincushion flower *(Scabiosa sp.)* and white Queen Anne's lace

**Tools:**

Floral scissors
Garden pruners
16- to 18-gauge wire cutters
floral tape

**Plant preparation:**

1. Cut a floret from the succulent plant, leaving a 3-inch stem. Strip off lower leaves and rinse with clean water.

2. Insert a length of 16- to 18-gauge wire into the base; cut wire so it is as long as the other flowers in your design.

3. Wrap the stem with green floral tape. "This gives your succulent a nice, clean look, which is especially nice for a hand-held bouquet," Susie says.

4. For tillandsias, or air plants, use a slightly finer wire and insert it through the plant's base without puncturing its root ball. Fold back two or three of the outer leaves along the wire "stem" so you can wrap them with the floral tape as described in Step 3.

5. Fill vase with water. Begin by placing the largest or most showy succulent so that it hangs over the lip of the vase.

6. Add other large flowers, including the dahlias and hydrangeas, rotating the vase as you work to achieve balance in form and color. Insert one or two medium-sized succulents or tillandsias so they are distributed throughout the bouquet.

7. Use soft filler, such as *Abelia* and oregano (or foliage of your choice) between the larger flowers. Remove any leaves that are under water.

8. Evenly distribute accent flowers, such as scabiosa and Queen Anne's lace.

9. Fill "empty" spots with more floral texture or color. Make adjustments like bending the wire stems to face succulents outward. The succulents will last up to a month or more; fresh-cut ingredients should last 5 days or more. Change water every two days.

# The Green Bouquet

**An eco-designer sources sustainable and uncommonly beautiful floral ingredients, while subtly educating her bridal clients that their choices do make a difference**

**Stacie Sutliff** left a successful marketing career with Amazon.com to follow the lure of flowers. She specializes in floral design for events and weddings. Through her studio, Blush Custom Floral, based near La Conner, Washington, Stacie sources her flowers from local farms where "I know that every stem I get has been planted, cared for and harvested in a way that maximizes its vase life and beauty."

Her eco-friendly approach often attracts bridal parties concerned about the environmental impact of their special occasion. Because of Stacie's proximity to the San Juan Islands, where hundreds of destination weddings take place each year, the carbon footprint of her bouquets is often as important to brides and grooms, as is the recycled paper used for invitations and locally-grown food served at their reception.

"I'm able to steer more of my customers toward what is locally and sustainably grown," she says. "To me, it just makes sense that if you're inspired by a beautiful place to get married, you'll want to know that the flowers you hold will not harm that place."

Blush Custom Floral's bouquets move customers beyond the ubiquitous hothouse options they might otherwise associate with wedding blooms. "When they ask 'Where does that flower come from?' I want to be able to say 'It comes from the farm down the road,'" Stacie says, her face brightening with a grin.

"I think it's the responsibility of florists like me to build the organic market. If we create beautiful things that our customers value and want to buy, again and again, then local flower farmers will naturally expand and innovate to meet that demand. Eventually, it will become economically feasible for them to grow some of those ingredients that today have to be imported or trucked in."

To illustrate the growing acceptance of locally-grown ingredients among her clients, Stacie offers this comparison: "In 2010,

**Above:** Stacie Sutliff draws from the botanical bounty of local flower farms to create her dreamy, romantic arrangements.

**Opposite:** An alluring peach and burgundy floral palette fills a cut glass vase. Stacey used locally-grown dahlias as the central flowers and repeated the dark color with wine-colored amaranth stems. Delicate stalks of Northern sea oats *(Chasmanthium latifolium)* lend movement and texture, while a touch of surprise comes from clusters of pinkish-white snowberries. The peach roses were conventionally grown, but Stacie prefers local roses when they are available.

Above: Stacie works closely
with her farm sources, often
incorporating their unexpected
ingredients into her work,
such as ornamental gourds,
artichokes (vegetable and
foliage), crabapple branches
and grapevines.

I sourced 30 percent of the flowers I used from local farmers. By 2011, that number went
up to 65 percent local flowers," she says.

## The Martha Factor

Using seasonality and local ingredients as their muse, "green" floral designers like Stacie
are clearly advocates for local flower farmers, who would otherwise be invisible to the
marketplace. Floral designers serve as a conduit between the farmer's field and the
glorious cascade of blooms that a bride holds in her hand.

   "What's difficult is 'un-doing' what brides think they want in a bouquet and helping
them discover the alternatives," she explains. Flowers in wedding magazines may be
beautiful, but they perpetuate the attitude that any and every flower is in season all year
long. For example, when a peony bouquet graces the cover of *Martha Stewart Wedding*
magazine, thousands of soon-to-be-brides fall in love with the look and want to carry
peonies down the aisle, even if it's the wrong time of year for that flower. Stacie addresses
these requests by saying to brides: "Here's what's in season, what's local – and less expensive than flying in peonies from New Zealand in the off season."

Terms like "local" or "sustainable" may conjure images of "a hippy-dippy bouquet in a Mason jar that your aunt put together," Stacie adds, "so I need to demonstrate to my brides how sophisticated local flowers can be. She has a vision and it's my responsibility to make her floral dream come true."

## Nature as Co-Designer

Stacie believes in creating uncontrived, natural-looking arrangements. She works closely with flower farmers to cultivate a mutually-beneficial relationship. Admittedly, it takes time and effort to find botanical diversity. Perhaps, she speculates, designers who have yet to tap the abundance of local fields and greenhouses may be complacent or satisfied with the "easy" route of buying imported alternatives.

Yet, to Stacie, the floral ingredients speak volumes about the quality and care with which they are selected. "When you see a floral arrangement that doesn't move you, it's pretty obvious. If you believe in seasonality, though, you're already taking design to the next level. Flowers that grow together, go together."

At the height of summer, in mid-July, Stacie gave us a demonstration of how she interprets this philosophy. We met at Jello Mold Farm, where she enjoys access to several acres of ingredients – flowers, foliage, fruit, grasses and vines. Using a square, shallow vessel of galvanized metal, ideal for a centerpiece, Stacie first inserted a loose ball of chicken wire inside, anchoring it with floral clay. She prefers this old-fashioned method of containing stems rather than florists foam, which is not biodegradable.

Stacie selected flowers at their peak of seasonal perfection. She used the chicken wire as her stabilizing framework for the arrangement, first placing branches of raspberry foliage, with their pleated surface and serrated edges; and stems from the aptly-named 'Coppertina' ninebark shrub and branches from its green-leaved relative, *Physocarpus opulifolius.* These stems obscured the chicken wire while their leaves cascaded attractively over the container's edge.

Working with the concentration of an artist at an easel, Stacie then placed coral-hued yarrow, 'Coco Puff' dahlias, roses with names like 'Sweet Antike' and 'Golden Celebration'. The unripe seed heads of *Achnatherum,* an ornamental grass, added delicate texture as a final touch. The design is abundant, anything but common, and thoroughly fascinating to the beholder.

"Just as people are thinking about locally- or sustainably-grown food, I'm hoping that they'll start thinking about their flowers that way," Stacie says. "The farmers are ready, willing and able to give us these products, but we, the consumers, need to create the demand."

**Above, from top:** Two arrangements from Blush Custom Floral demonstrate Stacie's embrace of the seasons, including a vase filled with raspberry canes, Chinese lanterns, wine-colored ninebark foliage, cockscomb and dahlias; and a low bowl featuring green and coppery ninebark foliage, coral-hued yarrow, 'Coco Puff' dahlias, 'Sweet Antike' and 'Golden Celebration' roses and Indian rice grass (*Achnatherum hymenoides*).

# TRADITION WITH A TWIST

## Arthur Williams draws from sculpture, Ikebana and the garden to create his iconic, over-the-top designs

"I've always approached things from outside the box," says **Arthur Williams**, Denver floral artist and owner of Babylon Floral Design. "Some of the textures that come together in my arrangements would never really happen in nature. It's as if aliens came to our planet and tried to do floral design."

One might easily conclude this from Arthur's arresting appearance, since most of his body is tattooed in patterns that he describes as "Hindu meets Japanese meets Art Nouveau with darker floral influences." The ink colors and piercings only tell part of who he is, for Arthur is also a gentle giant with a quiet voice, and a big grin for anyone who walks through the doors of Babylon Floral.

When we visited, David immediately went wild for the "vase" Arthur was using – a hollowed-out, gnarly section of a tree trunk. Having fabricated his own branch-vase for one of our garden club lectures, David appreciated Arthur's creativity.

The abstract arrangement of flowers and foliage was ideally suited for the container. Arthur started by inserting a cylindrical glass vase inside the salvaged piece of wood. To build the bouquet, he first used several pieces of ornamental rhubarb, with large green, ruffled leaves and fleshy flowering stems, harvested from his backyard. Next, he added locally-grown snowball viburnum – stems, leaves and powder-puff white flowers included – to lend a soft counter-point to the dinosaur foliage. Then he added several iris stalks, also from his garden, as well as locally-grown lilies for a punch of yellow. The design looked both effortless and sophisticated, and we really appreciated the care he took to source Denver-grown ingredients.

## Unconventional Design

Contrasting themes – hard-soft, masculine-feminine, or architecture-horticulture – are juxtaposed in much of Arthur's design work. In fact, the words Wabi and Sabi are tattooed across the tops of his hands "as a little reminder to be true to myself when I design," he says of the Japanese aesthetic with many interpretations, one of which is "imperfect beauty."

He opened Babylon Floral in 2004, drawing from a professional background that included work in greenhouses, landscaping and flower shops. Arthur grew up on a ranch, on Colorado's western slope, not too far from Aspen. A childhood spent food gardening morphed into an adult obsession with ornamental plants that now grow in his 7,000-square-foot city lot, although "I have a hard time letting go of pieces of my own garden for my design work," he admits.

While other florists rely on Teleflora or FTD orders for their business, Arthur quickly extracted himself from wire service floristry because "we had to make the kind of generic arrangements we would never be able to send our regular clients." Instead, he has followed his muse, relying on word-of-mouth and unsolicited customer raves on review sites like Yelp to attract new business.

Arthur's theatrical instinct for telling a story with flowers has made him famous in Denver art circles. For several years, he has collaborated with a local hair stylist, a makeup artist and male and female models to create fantastical botanical-inspired performance art. These magical, living creations often appear at gallery openings and have been featured at the Denver Botanic Gardens special events.

It can take hours to transform a model wearing a lightweight metal headdress onto which hair extensions, branches, vines, flowers and feathers are attached. Add makeup and a costume and the human form has become something else entirely.

Where does the inspiration come from? It might start with a sculptural stem, petal or twig, or a color theme, or a mythological character. "I draw from primitive cultures, from the need to adorn and the true ties with nature embodied by these cultures," Arthur says.

**Above:** A rustic, hollowed-out trunk becomes a natural "vase" when lined with a small glass cylinder that holds water.

**Opposite:** Arthur Williams, of Denver-based Babylon Floral Design, blends nature, architecture and his own quirky point of view to create over-the-top arrangements. He sources from local growers, foragers and greenhouses. Here, Arthur arranges long stalks of ornamental rhubarb that he clipped from his garden.

Outrageous as these creations are, they are influencing brides, who have begun to request "tamer" editions made with fresh flowers and feathers to wear as a wedding headpiece. "There's something appealing about the ephemeral quality of the work itself," he admits.

## The Local Question

Like many full-service florists, Babylon Floral tries to balance product availability and seasonality with the desires of its customers. For Arthur, who believes in using locally-grown ingredients as often as possible, it means taking the extra effort to find growers in his own community. "I love it when customers say: 'We want whatever you come up with,' because we might agree on a color scheme and size but that still gives me a lot of freedom to work with the flowers and foliage that are available in any given season."

Arthur feels that the design community has to do a better job of educating the floral consumer about seasonality and local product. For example, when one of his Denver clients told Arthur she wanted local and sustainable flowers for her January wedding, Arthur wished he could persuade her to reschedule to June, when local flower choices are much greater than during the winter. "People want to be sustainable, but they aren't really sure what that means," he concedes.

During Colorado's snowy months, Arthur gets inventive, basing his designs on twig and branch armatures to hold softer flowers and foliage. He sources much of the woody material, including dogwood, birch, curly willow, quince, forsythia, cherry and plum branches, "from a crazy local farmer named Patrick who just shows up with everything."

From late spring through early fall Babylon Floral sources from local flower farmers who specialize in zinnias, sunflowers, grasses and other seasonal crops. When winter frosts hit local fields, Arthur is able to obtain some flowers like lilies from nearby greenhouses. Otherwise he has to order from California flower farms or even South America. "It's sad," he says, "because Colorado used to be the carnation capital of the country until the 1980s, but it is all gone now."

Yet he continues to challenge convention, incorporating elements like painted branches and appropriating unusual, salvaged containers rather than predictable glass vases. "I'm continually drawn to local flowers rather than straight-stemmed, mass-produced ones," Arthur says. "They appeal more to my *wabi-sabi* aesthetics."

**Above:** Posing with "Dottie," his Jack Russell terrier, Arthur stands in front of larger-than-life photographs of models transformed by his beautiful floral headdresses.

**Opposite:** The finished tree-trunk arrangement, on display inside Babylon Floral, has a dramatic mix of snowball Viburnum, iris stalks, bluestem joint fir (*Ephedra equisetina*) and locally-grown lilies.

Local Grown Floral is Back

" *The kindness, the delicious, creative energy and unfailing generosity of the people we met just kept blowing us away; the way one ever-so-helpful flower grower at the Portland Flower Market introduced us to a floral designer, who then walked us over and effusively introduced us to yet another designer from another shop, telling us openly in her introduction just how much she admired the other's work. I mean, really, how often does that sort of thing happen in the world you live in? But there, within that energetic space and time-warp it happened again and again. There is something special going on in the floral world around Portland, Oregon, and here, for your edification and viewing pleasure is a first taste, a small initial sampling of those delightful faces and dancing eyes that so completely charmed us during our brief visit. We hope you will enjoy it . . ."*

— from David's blog post recapping our Portland visit.

# Botanical Wonderland

**Portland's floral design community offers a glimpse into a world where helping each other succeed means that everyone's business thrives. The flower consumer is the ultimate beneficiary of this collaborative spirit**

The Portland Flower Market occupies a sprawling warehouse in the city's industrial district just a few miles north of downtown. Although housed under the same roof as the region's flower importers, a 17,000-square-foot area is owned and operated by the Oregon Flower Growers Association to sell flowers, foliage and live plants direct to the designer. Founded in 1942, this farmer-to-florist market model is one that has recently been emulated in Seattle; its deep roots account for Portland's vigorous floral design community.

"Historically, most florists had a small greenhouse attached to their shops," Tom Cox, a bromeliad grower and OFGA president, said while we toured the market dedicated to the grower. Today, he continued to explain, the distinction between someone who grows flowers and one who owns a floral studio or retail shop is fairly delineated.

Here, people from both worlds do business as first-name friends, often meeting on a daily basis when the doors open at 6 a.m., year-round. Because the transaction occurs without a middleman, designers gain direct product knowledge from the person who actually grows the blooms. "I'm not just picking up ingredients at the market," says Adria Sparhawk, owner of Lavish, a studio specializing in weddings, events and corporate work. "I've also visited most of the farms. When a client points to a rose in my portfolio, I can tell her its story – and that creates a richer experience." Adria is often asked to share her market insights with local flower farmers. "It's a symbiotic relationship," she explains. "Growers ask me what style trends are coming – in both color palettes and popular flowers. It's nice to feel that I can influence what's planted next season."

Read on to meet some of Portland's creative floral designers who rely on the verdant ingredients grown on local farms.

**Above:** Adria Sparhawk, owner of Lavish, a Portland floral studio, greets Sandra Laubenthal of Peterkort Roses (right) and fellow designer Teresa Weis. The floral community seems to spontaneously convene most mornings at the Portland Flower Market where for decades florists have bought direct from area flower farmers.

**Opposite:** A banner proclaims "Local Grown Floral is Back," which sets the tone for an entire community of people who grow cut flowers and potted plants (like the holiday poinsettias we found on a December visit) – and the creative floral artists who transform the bounty of local farms into gorgeous bouquets and arrangements.

## Jennie Greene and Elizabeth Artis, Artis + Greene

The daughter of greenhouse florists, Jennie Greene designs with an edgy, modern floral style. She spent 18 years working as a sculptor and freelance designer in Tokyo – and New York City until soon after September 11, 2001. The event changed everything for Jennie, mostly affecting her health, which suffered due to exposure to toxins.

She decided to leave New York for Portland, where she used retraining funding from a nonprofit agency to open a flower shop. She converted a 20-foot shipping container into a pop-up retail setting – and located it for nearly a decade in a slot she rented in a downtown parking lot.

Jennie Greene Designs subsequently moved to two other storefronts, as Jennie attracted a loyal following of residential, restaurant and office clients who subscribed to her artfully-botanical bouquets of Oregon-grown flowers, stems, branches, bark and pebbles.

We met Jennie in 2010, while she was at the OFGA buying flowers with her 5-year-old daughter Ciana (who Jennie considers a third-generation floral designer). "She's already sold some of her work in the shop," announces the proud mother.

We also met Elizabeth Artis, a studio designer who freelanced for Jennie while also pursuing graduate studies in sustainable horticulture. We watched their comfortable friendship at play as they created arrangements and shared many of their eco-friendly and artistic techniques with us.

So it was no surprise to learn, less than a year later, that Jennie and Elizabeth formed a business partnership and opened a new flower shop called Artis + Greene. Located at the intersection of Broadway and Alder, in the heart of Portland's high-profile retail district, the 750-square-foot storefront has floor-to-ceiling paned windows, "so it looks like a greenhouse," Elizabeth enthuses.

Intense and thoughtful, with short brown hair tucked behind her ears, Jennie has more professional experience than her bubbly, redheaded colleague. Yet there is a refreshing attitude of mutual respect when you talk with the women.

"Jennie's background is so much more formal than mine, with her artistic training – while I have years of horticulture studies and have freelanced for a number of designers," Elizabeth explains of their rapport. "We complement each other's weaknesses and support each other's strengths."

**Above, from top:** Elizabeth Artis (left) and Jennie Greene pose with a towering, twig-and-orchid arrangement that Jennie has just created. The two women joined forces to open Artis + Green, a downtown Portland flower shop specializing in artful, local, chemical-free arrangements; Jennie often takes her young daughter Ciana with her as she shops for flowers, an early-morning ritual that has helped shape the 5-year-old's enthusiasm for floral design.

## Yin and Yang

The study of Ikebana and the trade of welding inform Jennie's work. She uses strict terminology to describe how flow, form, line and space compose her arrangements, some of which begin inside a traditional vase and end up draped or wrapped outside of it.

Like a restaurant's menu, her "design set" may change with the seasons depending on what the local flower farms are growing. But she refers to specific arrangements by name, such as: cascade, crescent, six-pack, or staircase.

There is an obvious asymmetry and pleasing precision to Jennie's designs that comes from her clever use of botanical ingredients. Anthuriums may be submerged under water, anchored by wire that's been wrapped around stones that were allowed to sink to the bottom of the vase. Or, in a glass saucer, a nest-like loop of red twig dogwood stabilizes lilies, tulips, roses, orchids and branches of red ilex berries that are tilted at desired angles for a stunning yet simple centerpiece.

Jennie demonstrated her techniques while making a wintry arrangement in a tall, slender glass cylinder. She began with long branches, their tips emerging nearly 24 inches above the vase opening. Next, she wrapped a band of birch bark around the vase and secured it with a fine, paper-wrapped cord called bind-wire. Then, she looped red huck branches, gathering and tying their shaggy ends to the birch piece. Other flowers added lush form and color,

including ilex, white lilies and delicate orchid stems, cut from a potted plant. The completed piece was sculptural and worthy of a pedestal in a gallery.

## A Natural Balance

The women showed us how they prepare stems before starting a design. Tricks like stripping away leaves and cutting the end of each stem at an angle using a clean, sharp knife extend an arrangement's vase life. Jenny and Elizabeth like to use willow branches, which have a slightly antiseptic quality that reduces the spread of bacteria in vase water.

Because she has chemical sensitivities, Jennie doesn't use floral foam or add preservatives to the vase water. Exposure to pesticides, fumigants and other chemical treatments is an ongoing problem for conventional florists, Elizabeth explains. "I get a skin rash when working with imported blooms that have been sprayed."

**Above from top:** Cultivating unique local sources for their designs is important to Jennie and Elizabeth. They rely on relationships with suppliers like this local forager who frequently arrives with a pickup truck of branches, boughs and foliage; Jennie uses a clean, sharp knife to cut woody stems on an angle, ensuring that the ingredients last longer in an arrangement.

**Next page:** Known for her architectural creations that blend ikebana and sculpture, Jennie's work is distinct and beautiful. This piece was achieved by wiring anthurium flowers to stones that sink to the vessel's base.

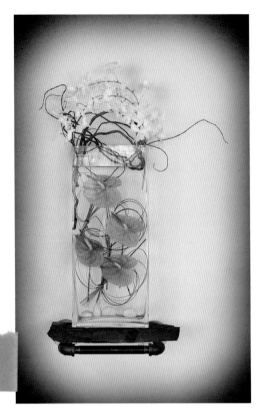

She admires the signature look of her partner's floral arrangements, noting that the store's reputation is built on "Jennie's distinct architectural design set." At the same time, though, she considers their individual styles to be complementary. "Jennie has been called 'the naked florist' because she picks off the leaves of almost any flower she works with to create something impactful and sculptural," Elizabeth laughs. "Whereas I would, if left to my own devices, be more free-form and bohemian, with lots of texture and greenery."

As the newcomer to this business, Elizabeth has contributed one particular floral style to the shop's menu of designs, which they jokingly call "weeds." "It's a wild and wavy mix of foliage and unconventional flowers that really communicates seasonality," Elizabeth says.

Says Jennie of her younger partner: "Elizabeth's use of color is painterly and complex. She creates soft palettes in surprising combinations of warm and cool tones that I would never try – but are simply magical." Where Elizabeth is the painter, Jennie is the sculptor. Combined, their rare talents delight loyal customers as well as a new population that is now discovering Artis + Greene.

The connection between her sculptural installations and floral design is evident, says Jennie, "but this is a lot easier than welding!" Unlike solid sculpture, flowers are both powerful and delicate, which makes one truly appreciate the of-the-moment quality of their work.

**"** *I get a skin rash when working with imported blooms that have been sprayed."*

— Elizabeth Artis, Artis + Greene

## Sarah Helmstetter and Alea Joy,
Solabee Flowers & Botanicals

Working out of a small storefront that's about the size of a building foyer in Portland's historic Kenton neighborhood, Sarah and Alea teamed up after both had managed other flower shops in town. Now creative partners, the women specialize in sustainable design for weddings and events. They source from local farmers, grow their own flowers and harvest ingredients from house plants, such as begonias, tillandsias, orchids and ferns.

Young and self-financed, Solabee's owners are resourceful: "We work with the economy we have now and with people's budgets," Sarah says. Her parents own 1½ acres of land east of Portland, filled with "wild and unusual plants," from which the designers glean foliage, branches and seed pods. "We are always looking at the ground, picking things up. We definitely like to forage," Alea explains. She describes their design style as "wild-crafting."

The women often guide customers to living plants as an even more sustainable floral option. "People are interested in things that are more permanent," Sarah explains. "Instead of a centerpiece, we suggest a planted terrarium or one of our living art pieces." To create the one-of-a-kind wall art, they have teamed up with a neighboring business called Salvage Works, which supplies Solabee with old tree roots, reclaimed branches, barn-siding or driftwood. Alea and Sarah plant succulents and tillandsias in the recesses and crotches of the salvaged wood. "Now, instead of hanging a flat-screen TV over the fireplace, our customer can hang this piece of art that is growing, living and changing," Sarah says.

It's not surprising that some of their fans want to borrow the concept from Solabee and make something similar, which doesn't seem to bother the designers. "People really do want to create things themselves," she says. "We try and encourage it, and if they want to buy the unusual plants or custom potting soil from us, that's okay, too."

Their youngest DIY customer, though, was a three-year-old girl whose parents planned her bouquet-making birthday party at Solabee. "We called them 'florists in the making,'" Sarah laughs. "It was really cool to help these little girls create their own designs."

Solabee's floral arrangements are often displayed in vintage containers, such as milk glass vases or antique bottles. A green rental program appeals to bridal parties who appreciate using the shop's vase collection for their wedding centerpieces, knowing the containers will be re-used by the next client.

**Above, from top:** Alea Joy, partner with Sarah Helmstetter in Portland's Solabee Flowers, holds a tabletop design in a vintage bowl. The flowers were grown locally and some of the foliage was harvested from a houseplant; a small arrangement features locally-grown lilies with imported orchids.

When we visited, Sarah and Alea had just finished creating a custom order: a sweet tabletop bouquet in a vintage footed bowl. Yes, it was nearly Christmas, and the ingredients were red and green, but any predictability stopped with the spotted begonia foliage, glossy magnolia leaves and maidenhair fern paired with red locally-grown Peterkort roses and California tulips. The entire design was installed in a bed of moss.

Many of Solabee's customers request locally-grown flowers in their arrangements; others are only beginning to understand what's in their hands. "We want people to know that local products are more affordable than you'd think," Alea says. "Especially if you are flexible! We ask the customer, 'What are your colors?' and from there we say, 'You're going to have to trust us.'"

### Pam Zsori, ink & peat

When you walk into ink & peat, Pam Zsori's eclectic, modern boutique in Northeast Portland, you'll want to browse the mix of hand-crafted and well-curated items for the home, including vintage collectibles and whimsical toys. But if you're there for the flowers, you will make a beeline toward the back of the 1,000-square-foot warehouse-like space where a full spectrum of botanical colors and forms is on display near a vintage chalkboard that lists flower varieties, like a restaurant's "specials" menu.

**Above, from top:** Sarah Helmstetter places a custom terrarium arrangement in the window of Solabee Flowers. The designers often use living plants in combination with cut flowers; at Portland's ink & peat, cash-and-carry flowers are displayed by color in simple Mason jars.

Blooms, branches and foliage are arranged by color, in individual glass vases, stair-stepped on tables by height. Hand-tied bouquets in Mason jars are affordably priced for cash-and-carry customers who snatch them up, beginning at $35. A nearby worktable accommodates Pam and her staff as they arrange and wrap custom arrangements. A counter sign reads: *We compost all floral cuttings.*

Pam, a textile designer who has worked for several top fashion companies, created ink & peat as a lifestyle-retail environment five years ago, "to reinvent my life and do the things I love," she says, describing her design transition from two-dimensional textile surfaces to three-dimensional floral bouquets. "Whenever possible, I like to source items that are sustainably-made and locally-grown," Pam adds.

Ink & peat's style is lush and textural, reminiscent of something gathered-from-the-garden, fields or woods. Here, sustainable design methods fly in the face of conventional ones and she refuses to use chemical-laden floral foam.

"Most floral designers use a green foam, brick-shaped material that you soak to hold water. The main ingredient of that product is formaldehyde, which is a known carcinogen," Pam says. "Florists who use it are touching the product day in and day out; the client might touch it when they take the arrangement apart; and then, ultimately, it's going to go into a landfill. It's not biodegradable, it's full of chemicals – so it's not a nice thing to work with."

Pam suspects that this throwback to the 1950s is still in use because of pure economics. "You can make something look much bigger and more expensive for less money if you use the foam," she says.

"A fresh arrangement done by hand, not in foam, has a lot more stems in it, which might make it more expensive than a traditional arrangement done in floral foam. To me, designs made in foam also look a lot stiffer."

Designers at ink & peat share their anti-foam techniques in the store's seasonal floral workshops. The popular three-hour classes cost $150 and introduce students to ingredients, color palettes and floral textures and green design methods. Each participant leaves with her own arrangement and a newfound confidence. "We teach people how to set up a grid of stems, starting with the foliage, so that it supports other blossoms," Pam says. "Our style is dictated by nature – I call it organized chaos – but there is also a certain order, rhythm and balance to the designs. Using a grid of stems to stabilize the flowers is really just physics."

**Above, from top:** Like a restaurant-style chalkboard featuring daily specials, ink & peat's menu lists flowers by name, with the corresponding stem-price; point-of-sale signage proclaims *We compost all floral cuttings.*

**Left:** Pam Zsori, owner of ink & peat, demonstrates her bouquet-making method that avoids the use of non-organic floral foam. The store's large worktable is frequently used for hands-on floral design classes.

# Organic Luxe

## Lily Lodge's A-list customers value organic bouquets, no matter where their ingredients are grown

A few years ago, floral designer **Ariana Lambert Smeraldo** of West Hollywood-based Lily Lodge gave her clients a reason to go green with a pre-Valentine's Day promotion that read *"Don't Poison the Ones You Love."*

"It had humor behind it, but the message gave me a reason to tell my customers why to buy organic," she explains. "Handling pesticide-ridden flowers, especially around children, isn't funny."

A mother herself, Ariana is emphatic: "Roses have the highest grade of pesticides. You are, in fact, sending poison when you send roses."

Enter organic roses, many of which are California-grown. "I love local roses that are grown in gardens, so their fragrance fills a room with the sweet smell one used to associate with flowers, before corporate floral mills began treating them like products on a conveyor belt," she says.

Since opening her luxury floral boutique in 2005, Ariana's organic message has inspired the red-carpet crowd that otherwise might give little thought to the toxic growing practices behind conventional bouquets. She sources pesticide-free blooms from small California flower farms or imports organic blooms from a handful of certified growers in South America, Europe, Israel and New Zealand.

Ariana has sleek blonde hair and a movie star smile. While she opened Lily Lodge with no formal floral design training, her successful background as a fashion stylist and retail executive for Bottega Veneta helped her carry it off with *élan*. The store's name was borrowed from her grandparents' summer retreat on the shores of Lake Katherine in the North Woods of Wisconsin.

**Above:** A floral bucket holds bunches of organic tulips next to the lid of a classic Lily Lodge flower box. The message inside reads: *Recycle! Bring this Box into Lily Lodge and Fill it With Our Organic Blooms for 50% Off.*

**Opposite:** Lipstick pink peonies, grown in New Zealand using certified organic methods, are perfectly arranged and ready for delivery to one of Lily Lodge's lucky customers.

**Above, from top:** The storefront windows advertise "Organic Flowers," sending an important message to shoppers who patronize this high-end West Hollywood neighborhood; organically-grown flowers and foliage in a full spectrum of colors and forms are displayed like artwork behind glass in Lily Lodge's custom walk-in cooler.

Ariana's focus on eco-savvy flowers is partly selfish. "I was pregnant for the first time when I'd only been open for a few months and that's when I understood on a personal level how non-organic flowers might not be good for an unborn child," she says.

As a businesswoman, she knew that offering the highest quality of flowers packaged elegantly or arranged in one-of-a-kind vintage vases would appeal to her celebrity clientele. Lily Lodge's dark green, oversized boxes come in several sizes and are made of recycled cardboard. The iconic packaging is reminiscent of timeless classics, like the glossy orange box by Hermes or Tiffany's robin's egg blue version.

Inside the lid of each Lily Lodge box is a message: *Recycle! Bring this Box into Lily Lodge and Fill it With Our Organic Blooms for 50% Off.* "This is my own recycling program," Ariana points out. She designed Lily Lodge with her husband Eric Nero

Smeraldo, a longtime actor and general contractor. Customers who enter their 1,300-square-foot shop on North Robertson Boulevard are greeted by a floral cooler like no other, an 11-by-16 foot wall of fresh flowers behind glass, reminiscent of a museum exhibit, with buckets of parrot tulips, bearded Irises, calla lilies, alliums, garden roses, hybrid ranunculus, sweet peas, anemones, French lilacs, New Zealand peonies, and Dutch hydrangeas arranged by bloom color.

The store is furnished like a salon with a vintage sofa, upholstered Louis XIV side chairs, a midcentury wood slab coffee table and a cowhide rug. A lodge-worthy antler chandelier hangs overhead. Dove gray side walls are lined with open shelving where rare vessels are on display – from a $50 midcentury pottery find to a $2,000 Peking glass vase from the Qing Dynasty. "The flowers, of course, are perishable, but afterwards, you still have a beautiful vase," Ariana points out. Continuing her quest to be as sustainable as possible, she never uses any container unless it is repurposed, recycled, vintage or antique.

Each Lily Lodge flower order is infused with lavish touches. When the recipient unties a pewter cotton ribbon and lifts the box lid, she won't find baby's breath or fern sprays, but she will be awed by 18 roses or dahlias or peonies arranged, row upon row, their individual stems hydrated in tiny water tubes, their plump heads nestled between layers of tissue. A card suggests specific floral care to ensure that the bouquet lasts as long as possible. The price? A box of hot pink peonies, organically grown in New Zealand, goes for around $350. "However, $75 still gets you more than a dozen certified organic roses," Ariana points out.

Writer and director Salim Akil ("Jumping the Broom," "Sparkle") appreciates Lily Lodge's "feminine, soulful flowers" that he sends to his wife, writer and producer Mara Brock Akil. "I'm not always the greenest person, but she certainly is," he says. "They aren't coming from a corporate chain, so I love the idea that these flowers have some depth to them."

By marketing her brand of organic floral design, Ariana believes she will effect change on a global scale. "I can't compete with Trader Joe's or Whole Foods," she says of the $10 or $20 mixed bouquets sold by area supermarkets. "But if I as a florist demand certified organic flowers, I believe I'm pushing the growers and wholesalers to respond."

She expects that the green floral marketplace will gain momentum, which is one reason why Ariana plans to expand Lily Lodge in the future. "Pretty soon, the term 'organic florist' will be obsolete, because all floral shops will be organic."

**Above:** Ariana Lambert Smeraldo, founder and owner of Lily Lodge, supplies organic flowers in luxury packaging. She's standing in the doorway of her elegant floral boutique and holding Lily Lodge's signature green box in which 18 gorgeous peonies are layered in tissue, their stems individually hydrated with water tubes.

## Do-it-Yourself Green

Eco-floral designer Ariana Lambert Smeraldo, owner of Lily Lodge, offers these floral gifting ideas:

• Buy local flowers or a potted plant from the farmers' market. Be sure to ask where they were grown and whether they were grown with organic practices.

• Wrap flower gifts in reusable fabric

• Repurpose a vintage vase to give your gift

# CHAPTER THREE

# The DIY Bouquet

*"I like to arrange as if each element was coming out of my garden, just as I harvested it. You have to see how the textures naturally come together to end up with a design that looks like a garden, rather than being manicured or tailored."*

**– Susie Nadler,**
The Cutting Garden
at Flora Grubb Gardens

# In a Paradise of Old Garden Roses

## David Perry introduces us to a world-renown rosarian, and walks with her in her magical garden of rare and fragrant roses

For most of us, the notion of a dozen roses still inspires a sense of romance, perhaps even extravagance and wealth. Imagine then how it might feel to have more than nine hundred of them, and I don't mean just nine hundred individual blooms. I mean nine hundred rose plants, most of them climbers and ramblers, each capable of pushing hundreds – and in some cases thousands – of scented blooms out into the world each growing season. This is the sort of wealth my friend **Anne Belovich** lives with daily.

Anne is an amazement, a bright-eyed woman in her eighties who has built up and who maintains what may be the largest collection of rambler and climber roses in the United States, with many specimens the only ones of their kind in the country.

She lives literally surrounded by roses on a fertile, rolling, five-acre plot of meadows and woodlands an hour north of Seattle, in a large, elegant home. It is a home that she and her beloved and too-soon-departed husband Max built with their own hands. Nearly everything about Anne seems deliberate and larger than life: her intellect, her generosity – the way she carries all that defines her within her slight, feminine frame. She is a photographer's dream. I nearly always make a portrait of her when I visit.

A few years ago, during one of my first visits of early summer, I was walking the garden paths with her when we fell quite naturally into the subject of bouquets. Anne's eyes began to dance as she told me how she used to cut bouquets of fresh roses for Max to take on his trips into town – gifts from their garden to offer up to a favorite waitress or the bank teller, or for the barber to bring home to his wife. She loved how much it pleased him to be able to offer such simple abundance to the people in his life. Though she was seldom along to witness the delivery of these floral gifts, she happily continued to cut bouquets on the mornings Max was headed into town – just for the pure pleasure and currency it gave him, she explained.

Spending time with Anne might convince you, as it has me, that stories have actual lives of their own and that they love being told, when they are told well. Anne is, among so many other things, a masterful storyteller.

"Did I ever tell you about the time I gave a bouquet of my roses to the governor?" she queried on a more recent garden visit, and began unfolding one of those delicious tales woven from her very intentional life.

"Well," she began… "we had a friend who was hosting a fundraiser for then-governor Gary Locke, and Max and I were invited to attend. Of course, I didn't want to show up empty handed, so I went out into the garden and cut a nice bouquet of some of my most fragrant roses, enough to fill a small plastic waste basket." She indicated the size with a gesture of her gardener's hands. "When I was finally introduced to the governor – I really liked him, you know – I extended my bouquet and said, 'Please give these to Mona (his beautiful wife), with my regards.'

"He leaned in, took a deep breath of their perfume and just beamed. 'Oh, thank you!' he said, taking the bouquet from me. 'We'll be sure to get your vase back to you.' 'No, please, don't even bother,' I said, 'I just go to my local discount store and buy several inexpensive little waste baskets at a time to give my bouquets away in. When the roses are done, you can use the waste basket for something else.'"

**Above, from top:** A ceramic bowl holds Anne's bouquet of alluring, fragrant, just-picked old roses; the arbor supports the apricot-buff blooms of 'Jacotte', a romantic French rose from the 1920s.

**Opposite:** Anne Belovich, rosarian, gardener, and occasional arranger of flowers.

**Previous spread:** Susie Nadler of The Cutting Garden, a floral studio at Flora Grubb Gardens in San Francisco, is an adventurous designer who likes to incorporate succulents and living plants into her bouquets of local flowers.

**Above, from top:** Anne's late husband Max built the allee, which she designed, to support some of the more than 900 roses in her collection; on a stroll through her floriferous landscape, Anne clips some favorite varieties for her simple arrangement.

**Opposite:** A dark pink rose of unknown origin is draped over a fence on Anne's property. She once thought it was classified as 'Debutante', but later, "I discovered that my plant was an imposter. I don't know what it really is, except to call it beautiful," she says.

And there you have a glimpse of the gracious and ever-so-pragmatic Anne Belovich.

Her story of the governor's bouquet gave me the perfect segue for a question I'd been cranking up my courage to ask her: "Would you consider cutting a bouquet or two of your roses for our book project?" I explained that I wanted to show our readers just how simple and doable a rose bouquet can be, quite apart from its implied grandeur – to show her walking out into her wonderland of a garden and cutting some of her very special and very old roses to put into a vase to bring indoors. Who better than Anne to help demystify the role of roses in our lives? Who better to counter the widely held belief that the only "real" roses are those sometimes ungainly and not always fragrant hybrid teas?

She thought about my proposition for a few minutes as we wandered between sun and shade, meandering along the perfumed rose- and clematis-covered allee she had designed and Max then built as her personal playground. Before agreeing to my request, she felt compelled to remind me that, really, she liked her roses best when left on their canes in the garden, and that she was not at all one for fussy, over-designed bouquets. Only then did she finally agree to play a bit in the garden, with my camera there to record her dance.

Five days later, I returned to the sanctuary of Anne's magical garden in the cool of a sunny, birdsong-filled morning. The roses were in full, opulent bloom. I wandered purposefully, cameras in hand, picturing each of her selections, this time recording her musings and her clipping and pairing process for the old-rose bouquets she was about to create.

As the birds continued to sing and as Anne stood backlit within her thoughtful garden, sharing just one more rose story, and then another, I could have pinched myself to be certain I wasn't dreaming. This wonderful, generous rosarian who allows me to call her my friend had just selected and cut some of her very rarest and most redolent roses at the peak of their perfection, and then turned them into her very own brand of unfussy, unassuming bouquets.

They were indeed fit for a governor . . . or perhaps even a queen.

## All about roses

**Old garden roses:** These are classes of roses introduced before 1867. Terms like heirloom, heritage and historic also refer to old roses, which may or may not date back as far. Favorites of Anne's include 'Charles de Mills', 'William Lobb' and 'Great Maiden's Blush'.

**Hybrid tea roses:** Hybrid Teas originated in 1867 from an accidental cross between a Tea and a Hybrid Perpetual. The resulting rose, 'La France', is considered to be the first hybrid tea and the beginning of the class of Modern Roses.

**Climbing roses:** These ambitious roses don't truly "climb" like an ivy, clematis or wisteria. Varieties are called Climbing Roses if they produce long enough canes to allow them to be tied or trained to a support so they appear to be climbing. Beautiful varieties in Anne's garden include 'New Dawn', 'Don Juan' and 'Climbing Iceberg'.

**Rambling roses:** While no longer recognized as an official category by the American Rose Society, the term Rambling Rose is still widely used by collectors and enthusiasts. A Rambler is generally considered to be a type of climbing rose with small flowers carried in clusters. Most are single-blooming, with wild roses in their parentage; a few may repeat their bloom like other modern roses. Some of Anne's cherished ramblers include 'Excelsa', 'Dorothy Perkins' and 'Albertine'.

*Not all nurseries or mail order catalogs carry old garden roses, although the ones listed here are commonly available. Anne recommends* www.helpmefind.com/roses/, *which provides information on roses, rose gardens and commercial sources.*

# ECO-FRIENDLY FLOWERS TO ARRANGE YOURSELF

## While sharing her know-how with flower lovers on both coasts, a young entrepreneur is changing the conventional role of the floral designer

**Bess Wyrick**, founder of Celadon & Celery Events, a New York-based eco-couture event design and floral decor company, thinks it's smart business to teach budget-conscious hostesses and brides how to create their own bouquets and centerpieces. The studio's popular workshops include demonstrations and hands-on participation "about the trends and techniques of the floral industry – while also having an eye on the environment," explains Bess, the company's twenty-something creative director, who exudes ambition and confidence.

It's important to Bess and her instructors that they share not just floral techniques but also insider florists' resources with their students. By doing so, they know that potential event clients will notice and appreciate their earth-friendly, chic aesthetic.

"We probably annoy a lot of people in our industry by teaching how to do these tricks of the trade, but we're in the middle of a recession and many people can't afford to do the type of weddings or events they used to," says Bess. A New Mexico native, she launched Celadon & Celery in 2009 after designing bridal gowns in San Francisco and working for one of New York's top floral studios.

Bess endorses an environmentally-savvy design approach that appeals to brides and special event clients alike, including the Kardashians, Vera Wang and Mayor Bloomberg, for whom she has provided flowers.

## Getting started

The studio's two-hour sustainable-design workshops typically go for $300. When Celadon & Celery expanded west to Los Angeles in 2011, Bess dropped the tuition to $125 for the first series of classes and used public relations and social media channels to promote them.

Overwhelmed by the positive response, she rented a photography studio in downtown Los Angeles and turned it into a classroom inspired by her loft-studio in New York's Chelsea Flower District. Bess hired a few local freelancers to help and ran three classes a day for three weeks. "In that time we taught floral design to 800 people," she marvels.

Hoping to experience the classes first-hand, we dropped by one Friday night. Photos of Celadon & Celery's eye-popping bouquets enlivened the otherwise stark white walls; upbeat dance music played on the speakers. Our own private flower market occupied the left side of the room, with all sorts of buckets containing a wow-worthy selection of fresh flowers and foliage. As students checked in, they snacked on hors d'oeuvres and sipped hot tea, eventually finding a spot along one of the waist-high worktables. Each station held a round glass vase, floral snips, bind-wire and a thorn-stripping tool. I found my own spot to join the class while David captured the energy of the room through his lens.

Where did these people come from? We met a fund-raiser for a local nonprofit and a film actress, among other (mostly female) students. Bess has her own theory about those who attend, often in pairs or trios with friends. "I think people are looking for an *experience* versus just going to a bar for a drink," she speculates. While she brushes her bangs out of her face, a delicate tattoo on the inside of her right wrist is revealed. It reads: *earth laughs in flowers.* It is a personal motto, surely, since laughing a lot is what Bess is good at.

**Above:** Bess Wyrick, founder and creative director of Celadon & Celery, is a young, enterprising designer who shares her knowledge with thousands of DIY students each year.

**Opposite:** With focused attention to the nuances of rose preparation, floral-design enthusiasts soak up Celadon & Celery's how-to tips. Many say that the hands-on workshop gives them new found knowledge and confidence to design their own arrangements.

With work aprons tied around our waists and everyone's vase filled with water, we eagerly grabbed clippers and eyed the fresh ingredients. Bess introduced each of the blooms and leaves, explaining its origin and variety as assistants distributed our "ingredients":

4 lime-green locally grown hydrangeas

5 bi-colored pink and cream certified organic 'Esperance' roses (grown in South America)

2 gray-green sprays of Dusty Miller foliage

3 California-grown dahlias

6 burgundy ti leaves from Hawaii

10 variegated blades of lily grass, also from Hawaii.

Even though each of us used the same design "recipe" and set of flowers, no one felt deprived of creativity, since there was plenty of wiggle room to experiment as we worked.

"Think about filling a vase of flowers like you're building a puzzle," Bess explained as she began to demonstrate with a contemporary glass cylinder. "You start with the border and then fill in toward the center," she said, swiftly filling her vase as she demonstrated how to "line" it with two of the burgundy-and-green ti leaves so that their streaks of color disguise the other stems inside. Rather than poking stems into the florists' foam she hates to use, the designer showed us how to create an interior grid with each flower stem crossing the next. First, we arranged the hydrangeas; then, we inserted the gorgeous roses among them, trying out a designer's trick by threading a rose stem through the center of the fluffy hydrangea – like topping whipped cream with a cherry. By folding over the long ti leaves and securing their tips to their stems with some wire, the burgundy foliage soon resembled loops of ribbon on a gift box. There were plenty of gaps to integrate silvery Dusty Miller leaves and magenta dahlias, each addition upping the glamour of the vase. Several slender blades of the otherwise ordinary lily grass, looped and tied like the ti leaves, created the sparkling finale.

Pretty soon, each of us gazed proudly at our floral masterpiece, sharing smiles and words of encouragement. It was no surprise to witness more than one adult snap a photo of her finished bouquet to post on Facebook or Twitter. I loved how polished and chic my arrangement looked. "At the end of the class, no one wants to leave," Bess jokes.

I asked Sash Ramaswami and Robinne Lee, who came together with another friend, what prompted them to sign up. Sash learned about the workshop through social.com, a daily deal site, she said. "I have always wanted to have great-looking flower arrangements, but I never knew what to do. No matter how pretty my flowers were, they looked awful in a vase." For each, the short class helped nurture their inner floral designer. Sash sent me an email message a few weeks after the workshop, writing: "A friend came over and asked me if it was my birthday. She saw the arrangement I had made and said it looked so professional that she thought someone had sent me flowers. Mission accomplished!"

Similarly, Robinne savored the hands-on class, describing it as "the perfect girls' night out." While she had never tried arranging flowers before, Robinne always admired the skill in others. "I think I can do this for myself or friends now," she said.

## Designer secrets

For its New York design commissions, Celadon & Celery buys from Long Island, Connecticut and New Jersey growers. The studio composts all greenery and delivers arrangements by bicycle or on foot.

Celadon & Celery's direct relationship with farms gives the studio its leading edge, Bess feels. "We're helping establish the market by predicting what brides are going to want. We can be confident placing an order for 5,000 dahlias because we know who is growing them. We've definitely bypassed the Manhattan middlemen and have gone straight to the farmers."

In Los Angeles, thanks to an abundant supply of California-grown local blooms and some imported ingredients bearing the Veriflora label (indicating sustainable growing practices), Bess filled the L.A. pop-up studio with a fresh explosion of botanical variety. It was easy, since the Los Angeles Flower District, one of the largest wholesale flower markets in the country, was located just blocks away.

By giving students an original experience with a nod to the environment, Celadon & Celery has tapped into a visceral desire to connect with nature, take creative risks and try something they may have never done before – arrange flowers with intent rather than just tearing off the cellophane wrapping and shoving a bunch of stems into a vase.

"The word 'eco' has a bad reputation, implying something weedy," Bess says. "But we're creating flowers that are sophisticated, chic and tailored. We often tell our students to have fun with their arrangements, to be imaginative and to get in touch with their inner child."

**Above, from top:** Bess demonstrates a trick with roses: She sometimes folds back the outer petals of a long-stemmed rose to make the flower head appear fuller; according to Bess, male students like Miles Clark are not a rarity. "Guys enjoy learning how to design flowers as much as women do," she says.

## Tips from Celadon & Celery

Bess wants students to use a sustainable approach and learn the skills to make their own wedding or event flowers. Here are some of the studio's tricks and techniques:

- Divide floral ingredients into three categories based on form: Doming flowers, such as hydrangeas, dahlias, roses and other large, full blooms; Line flowers, such as calla lilies and tulips; and Filler, such as baby's breath, goldenrod, daisies or soft foliage.

- Calculate the number of stems your vase will hold by multiplying the vase diameter by 10. For example, a 6-inch-wide vase opening will hold up to 60 stems.

- Start with a thoroughly clean vase. "Your flowers will last 30% longer," she says.

- Use a variety of "green" arranging materials inside your vase. Old-fashion flower frogs, pincushion-style frogs used by Ikebana designers or loosely-formed chicken wire are each an excellent alternative to green florists' foam, which Celadon & Celery's staff calls "cancer-on-a-stick" because it has so many toxic ingredients.

- Stems can also be stabilized by taping a grid over the vase opening or making a natural one by angling flower stems to support each other.

- Set water temperature depending on the type of ingredients: Branches and woody material prefer warmer water; flower stems prefer cooler water.

- Re-hydrate some wilting blooms, including hydrangeas. Dunk their heads in tepid water for 5 to 10 minutes to refresh them. If your flower has a hollow stem, like a calla lily or amaryllis, submerge the entire stem to fill it with water. Plug the opening with a piece of cotton ball. The designer uses this trick for gala events when she hangs flowers upside-down from the ceiling.

- Determine whether a rose is right for your arrangement. The technique is a lot like squeezing fruit in the produce department to see if it's ripe. "Gently press the head of your rose," Bess suggests. "If it has the consistency of an orange, with a little give to it, then it's perfect."

- Wrap, secure or tie stems in place with bind-wire, one of her favorite tricks. The thin wire has a waxy coating and comes in a dark green or natural brown finish.

**Above:** Bess kneels in front of a class photo (that's Debra on the far right). Everyone left with two arrangements and the self-assurance to use professional techniques in the future.

**Opposite:** Our bouquets were based on a joy-inducing palette of greens and pinks. The ingredients included California-grown hydrangeas, dahlias and Dusty Miller; foliage from Hawaii; and certified organic roses from South America.

# Shopping the Supermarket

**With her commitment to local flowers and those who grow them, Kristen Parris has single-handedly changed how one grocery chain stocks its flower department to serve a loyal customer base**

**Kristen Parris** has trained her customers at Ballard Market to ask where their flowers come from. Blooms, branches, foliage and other ingredients grown on Pacific Northwest flower farms are wrapped up in natural Kraft paper to differentiate them from imported varieties, which have clear cellophane wrapping. Even at a glance, the packaging tips off supermarket shoppers. Attractive signage also clues them in, with tags that read: *"Multiflora rose hips from Oregon,"* or *"Crabapples from Jello Mold Farm."* Kristen is committed to sourcing product from local farms and marketing the bouquets and bunches as "Locally Grown," which has resulted in an increase in sales during the summer months when, traditionally, daily sales slow down as customers' own gardens are in bloom.

Her eyes sparkle with glee as she shows off her floral department at Ballard Market, in one of Seattle's hip, artsy neighborhoods. If it weren't inside a bustling market, tucked between the cash registers and the ATM machine, the floral department could easily be a small neighborhood flower shop, which is how Kristen and Danielle Bennett, her assistant and fellow local-flower evangelist, treat the compact space. After 26 years in the floral industry, it's refreshing to see that Kristen is still energized by her craft while also mentoring Danielle as her protégée. "Danielle's incredibly talented," Kristen says proudly.

She is repeating the pattern of her own apprenticeship, which began when Kristen was 16 and took her first job at the only flower shop in Maple Valley, Washington. An outer suburb of Seattle today, Maple Valley has agricultural and logging roots. It was there, on her family's farm where they raised beef, various berries and stone fruit, that Kristen gained a strong work ethic and an affinity for anyone who makes their living from the land.

Recalling that first job, she says, "While I always enjoyed the flower shop's unusual tropical flowers or perfectly-coiffed orchids that were imported from Thailand, I realized then that I just wanted to walk into the woods and gather moss from the forest floor. Even as a teenager, I felt connected to nature."

## Local flora

When Kristen later worked for prominent flower shops in Bellingham and Seattle, she sought out local flower farmers and asked to buy from them. "I wanted to connect with people who grow," she recalls. "I would go to the farmers' markets, hand out my cards and say to the vendors, 'I have to know your story; I have to see your farm.'"

Her children were still young when in 1995 Kristen walked into Ballard Market, a neighborhood supermarket that's part of the six-store, Seattle-area Town & Country chain. It was less than five miles from her home and she liked its vibe. Her experience got her hired. And since then, her passion and vision (not to mention support from various store directors) have redefined how Ballard Market's floral department operates.

Working alongside Danielle as the two prepared arrangements for an upcoming holiday weekend, Kristen explained her philosophy. Whereas most grocery chains view flowers as a perishable commodity, she understands that behind every bunch of blooms is a family farm. "All of my conventional wholesale sources know that my number one priority is local," Kristen says, glancing up to make sure we get her point. "They would

**Above, from top:** Kristen Parris (left) and Danielle Bennett run their supermarket floral department like a welcoming neighborhood flower shop. These autumnal mixed bouquets are wrapped in brown Kraft paper, signaling to Ballard Market's customers that the flowers are local.

**Opposite:** Based in Seattle, Ballard Market uses point-of-purchase signage to promote the importance of locally-sourced mixed bouquets and bunches of blooms.

never try to sell me dahlias in the summer when they know I'm buying hundreds of bunches from local flower farms."

Yet, due to the short production season of many locally-grown ingredients, Kristen can't completely abandon importers altogether. "The traditional wholesalers know to call me *after* the local season is over," she says. But with the arrival of frost, Kristen still stocks whatever seasonal goodies the area growers can harvest, such as rosehips, ornamental grasses, seed heads, colorful twigs and evergreens boughs.

## Kindred spirits

Kristen met another co-conspirator in 2007 when Diane Szukovathy pulled her Jello Mold Farm truck into Ballard Market's parking lot hoping to sell flowers. When Diane opened the doors, "the air couldn't get in my lungs fast enough," Kristen recalls. "I think I cried."

The women's connection was instant and both agree that it has been mutually beneficial. When Diane and several other Northwest flower farmers launched the Seattle Wholesale Growers' Market in 2011, they invited Kristen to serve on their board. Having a merchant who understands the

flower-buying public has been invaluable to the local farmers, Diane says. "I don't know if our farm would still be here and thriving without Kristen's support," she maintains. "There is no substitute for her level of caring and trust. We've come so far from how flowers used to be bought and sold in this country, and it takes people like Kristen to help bring things back into balance. She works just as hard as the farmers with her vision and commitment to educating the public."

It is fitting to call Kristen a local-flower evangelist. "I want to teach farmers how much the product they grow is worth," she explains. "That's the only way they can made a decent living." To illustrate her point, Kristen describes what happened when Town & Country established $7.98 as the chain's retail price of a dahlia bunch in 2011. Depending on the size of the bloom, each bunch included 5 to 7 brilliant flowers in tones from pastel to jeweled. One local grower had regularly charged Kristen a wholesale price of $2.35 per bunch, "and we were buying 800 bunches a week from this guy," she marvels. When Kristen tried to give him a $1-per-bunch "raise," based on the new retail price, the farmer worried that the boost would somehow leave his fields filled with dahlias that wouldn't sell.

"I had to tell him that it was okay to raise his price," she says, shaking her head. "You know, we had a banner year for dahlias, and so did he."

## Seasonally speaking

With so many who live in the neighborhood shopping at Ballard Market almost daily, Kristen has developed extensive friendships with her customers. It's not uncommon for someone to stop by the floral department before hitting the dairy case or cereal aisle, plunk down a $20 bill and ask Kristen or Danielle to "make up a local bouquet for me."

Recently, she surprised her regular customers when she began selling locally-grown tulips – during the off-season. Kristen was stocking bunches of fall-toned hothouse tulips from Washington Bulb Co., a large grower of flowering bulbs and cut flowers from Mount Vernon, Washington. But she took some flak from customers who for years have heard her insist they buy only field-grown tulips. "I've been eating crow," she jokes. "But these tulips *are* local and they make a nice hostess gift."

Watching customer buying patterns gives this veteran an optimistic outlook. "I'm intrigued that more people are asking where their flowers came from." When there's a local flower advocate like Kristen, one who loves to tell the story of the farmer and inspire customers to listen, the future for local flowers is a rosy one. And as more retail florists like Kristen source their flowers locally, it means flower farmers can plant and grow even more uncommon and gorgeous crops.

**Above:** Just-delivered buckets filled with mixed bouquets of perennials, annuals, grasses and even fruit from local farms stand ready to wow Ballard Market's floral customers.

**Next spread:** The floral palette featured in Julie's bridal and bridesmaids' bouquets appears as centerpiece elements for the post-ceremony gala dinner. The banquet tables are adorned with an alternating display of succulent-planted wood boxes and groupings of dahlias, succulents and other flowers in glass canning jars.

# CHAPTER FOUR

# Celebrations
# & Festivities

*"As with food, if you start
with good ingredients –
in this case, gorgeous blooms –
things generally take care
of themselves."*

**– Julie Chai,**
*Sunset* magazine garden editor
and DIY bride

# JULIE AND GEORGE GET MARRIED

**A top garden editor creatively plans her dreamy, highly personal nuptials to her beau – with locally-grown flowers, of course**

On a warm July afternoon, music filled the air with Lauren Hill's rendition of "Can't take my eyes off of you." A beaming bride crossed the vast lawn and approached a towering grove of redwood trees where 170 family members and friends gathered to witness the ceremony. Her mother on one arm and her father on the other, **Julie Chai** smiled at her longtime sweetheart **George Lee**, his face expressing similar joy. Julie embraced her parents and then laughed, as George bounded over and took her arm in his.

She wore a strapless, floor-length ivory gown of lace over satin. Off-white chiffon blossoms graced the nape of her neck and dark brown tendrils framed her face. And in her hands, Julie held coral, apricot and pink dahlias in a bouquet she created from flowers picked just days earlier. "I'm crazy about dahlias – the colors are so vibrant and rich, happy and cheerful," she says of her floral inspiration. Julie and George wanted to have a wedding of their own creation, and when it came to selecting the flowers, Julie says, "I knew that these dahlias would practically design themselves."

For a decade, Julie has produced, written and blogged about gardening topics as an editor at *Sunset.* The popular magazine reaches nearly 5 million readers per month and Julie frequently appears in its how-to articles and online videos. Her charismatic eyebrows lift when she smiles, and it always seems to me that Julie is about to do something gleeful and spontaneous – and her friends, of course, want to be a part of it.

In a way, Julie and George's decision to marry was somewhat spontaneous, even though many of their friends had waited more than a decade for the day to come. Both grew up in the Bay Area

**Above:** For their garden wedding, George Lee and Julie Chai wanted every aspect to be personal, local and meaningful – including their bouquet and boutonniere that Julie designed and arranged.

**Opposite:** Before the ceremony (no wedding ring yet!), Julie holds a vibrant mix of locally-grown dahlias in shades of pink, apricot and coral. She propagated the succulent ingredients and grew the perennials in *Sunset* magazine's test garden. Together, they add up to a stunning bridal bouquet.

and attended the University of California at San Diego, at the same time. But they didn't meet until after graduation when a mutual friend invited Julie to join a trip he'd already planned with George and several other friends. Julie and George became a couple six months after that, and for 12 years they were content simply being committed to each other. "But on a vacation to Yosemite we got inspired to get married – it just felt right," Julie says. "Ironically, it was the first trip we'd been on when people weren't asking us whether we were going to get engaged while we were away, and we decided to go for it."

Julie planned her wedding as if producing a huge photo shoot. George, a product manager for Facebook, was as involved as was his bride, saying, "We really wanted the day to reflect who we are." And lucky us – we tagged along to document the process. From the start, the couple intended it to be a "hands-on" event, with all the ingredients – including the bouquets, centerpieces and party favors – coming from people they knew and loved.

**Above, from top:** Mason jar vases filled with coral and pink dahlias hang by wire looped over the backs of chairs – adorning the outdoor "aisle" for the processional; George Lee shows off his boutonniere, made with love by Julie.

**Opposite:** *Graptopetalum paraguayense* is a succulent blue-gray rosette that complements vivid orange and pink dahlias. Julie appreciates the succulent's petal-like form.

## Local and personal

With a commitment to all things local, Julie and George chose *Sunset's* Menlo Park, California, headquarters as the venue for their ceremony on July 23, 2011 (use of the property for a private wedding is a rare privilege extended to employees). "I loved the idea of a backyard wedding, and to me, *Sunset* feels like a big backyard. The building and gardens are very special to me – they have so much soul," Julie points out. Architect Cliff May, father of the California ranch-style home, designed *Sunset's* offices in 1952. Thomas Church, dean of Western landscape architects, designed the 7-acre grounds on land that was originally part of a grant to Don José Arguello, governor of Spanish California in 1815. Together, the architecture and gardens exemplified the ultimate 1950s indoor-outdoor Western lifestyle – and while *Sunset's* editorial focus now addresses the 21st century, that theme still resonates.

The breathtaking setting meant that decorations were practically unnecessary. Natural wood chairs were positioned to face the ceremony location, a sheltering grove of redwoods. Nearby, a majestic coast live oak provided a canopy where tables were arranged for dinner – with large paper lanterns adorning the branches that afternoon. *Sunset's* picture-perfect outdoor kitchen, featured in many of the magazine's cooking and entertaining stories, was the ideal spot for post-ceremony cocktails and toasts.

Julie created two "vision" boards to map out with photographs and words how the wedding looked and felt in her mind's eye. "We posted words like *personal, casual, joy-filled* and *meaningful,* along with color swatches and images of flower arrangements, decor and cakes, for inspiration."

Her favorite dahlias determined the color palette, since Julie knew these quintessential summertime blooms would dazzle against her bridesmaids' subtle gray cocktail dresses and the men's charcoal suits and apricot ties. She encouraged her sister-in-law and four close high school and college friends to each wear a dress style of her own choosing. "Each is so special to me and I wanted them to look like themselves," Julie explains.

In her editor's role, Julie scouts gardens and interviews fascinating plant experts all around the West, so it wasn't difficult to conjure botanical inspiration. "I hoped to use at least some flowers that were grown on-site at *Sunset* since I'm so sentimental about these gardens," Julie says. So she found a way to incorporate a selection of what was growing in the test garden and would be blooming in July, including yarrow, lamb's ears and Shasta daisies, as well as several dahlias.

Knowing that making nearly 40 vases and six bouquets required many more flowers than she herself could grow, Julie contacted Corralitos Gardens, a small dahlia grower located south of Santa Cruz. "Even as a gardener, the idea of growing all my own wedding flowers was a little daunting. It's hard to know if you'd plant the right amount or if the flowers you want would bloom at exactly the right time."

She was familiar with owner Kevin Larkin's reputation as one of the best dahlia producers around (see story, pages 116-119). "We've trialed a number of his dahlias over the years, and loved all of them," Julie explains. "And it was important to me that I bought my flowers from someone I knew who was nearby." She studied the varieties pictured in Corralitos Gardens' online catalog to come up with a spectrum of bloom colors. "Kevin also gave me expert advice, such as knowing which dahlia varieties hold up longest when cut." Working from centerpiece samples to calculate how many individual stems she would need, Julie pre-ordered a mix of 300 dahlias. Kevin harvested them in advance and two days before the ceremony, the bride and two of her attendants made a memorable road trip to Corralitos Gardens, filling Julie's car to the brim with the breathtaking blooms.

In addition to the flowers grown at *Sunset* and Corralitos Gardens, Julie propagated hundreds of succulents to use as her third floral element. She borrowed creative techniques from Susie Nadler

(The Cutting Garden at Flora Grubb Nursery) and Baylor Chapman (Lila B. Flowers & Events), two Bay Area floral designers she had met through the magazine. "I *looove* their designs and I looked to their work to inspire my bouquets," Julie says.

Using succulents required advanced planning. "I started taking cuttings from my plants six months before the wedding. By July, we probably had 350 of them, including ones from an echeveria plant that was given to me by my very first gardening mentor, which came from cuttings she took from her mother's plant 30 years ago," Julie raves. She cherishes the continuity of a plant that became part of the bouquet she clutched in her hands as well as an ingredient in the boutonniere pinned to the lapel of George's elegant charcoal suit.

"I do feel that, as with food, if you start with good ingredients – in this case, gorgeous blooms – things generally take care of themselves," she explains. "Trying to be flexible was one of the most important parts of planning our wedding. As a result, everything came together so much better than we could have ever anticipated. We wanted spontaneity. We wanted to let magic to happen on its own."

**Above, from top:** Five of Julie's closest girlfriends, including her sister-in-law, served as bridesmaids. Each woman personally selected the dahlias and other flowers for the bouquet she held; the handmade boutonnieres for George and his groomsmen contained one small succulent echeveria and the fern-like foliage of Dusty Miller *(Centaurea cineraria)*.

**Following spread:** With her joyous bouquet clutched in her hand and happiness expressed on her face, Julie is captured during a pre-wedding moment.

## How can I help?

Julie and George wanted every piece of their wedding to tell a personal story or connect them with someone dear. They went for high-touch, and included many hands (and hearts) in their special ceremony:

- Rev. Julianne Stokstad, who officiated the wedding, is a friend of the Chai family – and herself an avid gardener.

- Amy Machnak, *Sunset's* recipe editor, made the four-tiered coconut rum cake and used extra dahlias to embellish it.

- Jess Chamberlain, *Sunset's* market editor, served as the "style director" and oversaw the decor.

- Brianne McElhiney, *Sunset's* assistant program manager, served as wedding coordinator for the day.

- Spencer Toy, *Sunset's* digital imaging manager, took the wedding photographs.

- Mauricio Cuellar, a high school friend of Julie's who is a DJ, provided music.

- Other friends helped create seating cards, assembled favors and made additional desserts as their gifts to the bride and groom. A sign at the desserts bar read: "All desserts are homemade with love!"

- Feel Good Foods Organic Catering, the local caterer, created an organic, seasonal menu.

## Hands-on flowers

A simplified plant palette made Julie's DIY floral design easier to accomplish. It also made the flowers look more stylish.

With hundreds of individual dahlias to choose from, Julie and each of her bridesmaids personalized their bouquets, stem by stem and I had fun helping them. We mixed-and-matched various forms, colors and sizes of dahlias, using enough blooms to fit comfortably in the hand when gathered. After forming a balanced, dome-shaped grouping of dahlias, we added accent flowers – several sprigs of dark pink yarrow and velvety gray lamb's ears. For a finishing touch, the succulent "flowers" were carefully inserted into each arrangement (the short stems of the cuttings gained length from a slender wood skewer secured with floral tape). More floral tape was used to wrap the entire bouquet "handle" and hold all the stems together. The bouquets were stored in jars of water until just before the ceremony, when we secured the stems with pewter-gray satin ribbon.

The banquet table centerpieces included groupings of differently-sized canning jars that contained lush arrangements of dahlias, succulents, Shasta daisies and yarrow blooms. At the last moment, two of Julie's bridesmaids used wire to hang dahlia-filled jars from a number of chairs lining the grassy aisle – a whimsical gesture that simply adorned Julie and George's processional.

Hi-Dong Chai, Julie's father, used scrap wood to construct a dozen square planting boxes. After Julie whitewashed the exterior of each box, she planted them with a fanciful array of unusual succulents – a gift from friend Robin Stockwell of Succulent Gardens, a specialty nursery.

"Robin's plants are stunningly beautiful," Julie says. "And I wanted people to see them close up." Like jewelry cases with their lids removed, these planters also served as centerpieces that Julie and George later gave as gifts to members of the bridal party.

## Party favors

Every guest received a living thank-you gift from Julie and George: a chartreuse or pale blue succulent that they transferred from growing trays into small glass flowerpots the week before the wedding. Each favor had a wooden plant tag with a link to a plant-care web page that George created. *"We gave you a sweet little succulent to take home because they're super easy to grow – and they eventually multiply, so you can give them to your friends! Your plant is the baby of one that Julie got from gardening friends over the years and we hope that you'll continue to pass them on."*

**Above, from top:** On the day prior to the wedding, Julie (right) and Ughetta Manzone assembled their flowers; Julie and George propagated and planted a miniature succulent for each wedding guest as a personal memento of the day.

**Opposite:** Amy Machnak, *Sunset's* recipe editor, made the four-tiered coconut rum cake and adorned it with pink and coral dahlias.

# Swoon-Inducing Dahlias

**One trip to the dahlia farm and you'll be hooked on this beloved summer classic – for the cutting garden, your vase or bridal bouquet**

Best known for its mail-order business selling dahlia plants to gardeners and growers, Corralitos Gardens is also a seasonal flower farm on the central California coast, where row upon row of alluring specimens lure visitors to admire their uncommon forms and colors, both subtle and intense in hue. And if you live nearby, it's possible to carry home an armload of just-picked dahlias for your dinner party or wedding.

Before starting their mail-order business, **Kevin Larkin** and **Karen Zydner** had been growing dahlias as a hobby for a few years. In the mid-1990s, Kevin recalls, "local florists didn't want them. Now I can sell every stem I grow to designers and their brides."

Is the dahlia's rise in popularity due to changing tastes among floral enthusiasts who now appreciate its beautiful symmetry? Or is it thanks to a newfound hunger for the vivacious, attention-grabbing colors? Some floral designers prefer dahlias because of their versatility – they are equally suitable for old-fashioned, nostalgic arrangements and architectural, modern ones. "All I can say is that they fill people with pleasure," says the man who has received countless thank-you letters and photographs from grateful wedding parties who purchased their dahlias from Corralitos Gardens.

Indeed, this long-blooming star of the summer perennial garden offers something to entice any bride or party host. The dahlia hails from highland areas of Mexico and Central America. Experts say that centuries after cuttings of three species of the flower were brought by plant explorers to Spain, the parentage of tens of thousands of today's hybrids can likely be traced to those original plants. Hardy in frost-free regions, the dahlia is a member of the daisy family (Asteraceae). Dahlia tubers, those sweet-potato-looking clumps with an "eye" at one end, are actually modified stems that store nutrients and water underground while sending up show-stopping blooms on tall, leafy stalks. The flower itself is formed by many petal-like "ray" florets arranged around a center of "disk" florets.

Kevin and Karen formed Corralitos Gardens as a retail mail-order business in 2002. They purchased a 30-acre farm in California's Santa Cruz County, located about five miles inland from the Pacific Ocean and a few miles from their residence. With backgrounds in agriculture, the couple capitalized on a unique propagation method that allows them to ship high-quality, easy-to-plant dahlias (rather than a yet-to-sprout tuber) to gardeners around the country between March and June. Customers in 42 states gobble up 15,000-plus plants each spring, choosing from the 400 varieties pictured in Corralitos Gardens' online catalog.

In addition to producing dahlia plants, Corralitos Gardens devotes one acre to field-grown varieties for cut flowers, supplying area floral and event designers all season long – from July through late September. A table with a huge umbrella operates as Corralitos's self-serve flower stand at the entrance to the nursery.

**Above, from top:** Glistening in the sunshine are rows and rows of some of the 300-plus dahlia varieties grown for cutting by Corralitos Gardens. Just two days before her nuptials, Julie Chai visited the flower farm to select her favorite dahlias for centerpieces and bouquets.

**Opposite:** Sheltered by several majestic live oaks that dot the coastal California flower farm, Julie works with Kevin Larkin to sort dahlias by color and size.

Customers come from a 50-mile radius to partake in a summertime ritual of choosing a hand-tied bunch of dahlias and dropping a five-dollar-bill into the can.

Many DIY brides, like Julie Chai, purchase directly from Corralitos Gardens. "Dahlias are a great cut flower, and your best source is to go right to the grower," Kevin says. "They are ideal from a local standpoint because they're somewhat ephemeral and do not ship well." That's not to say cut dahlias are short-lived. "When you buy direct from the grower, your dahlias should last at least a week in the vase," he maintains. Kevin appreciates customers like Julie who have a flexible wish list in a range of dahlia bloom colors. That's because Corralitos Gardens has great diversity – 300 named varieties are grown for cutting – but not huge quantities of any single one. Some wedding parties plan far enough in advance to actually order the plants and grow them themselves, timing it so as to harvest their own backyard blooms for a late summer ceremony.

Not just price, but quality and freshness, are factors influencing the worth of a locally-grown dahlia bouquet. While a cellophane-wrapped bunch of imported roses might seem like a bargain at $9.95, once you bring it home, you may cease to be wowed, since those roses lack scent and seem almost generic. "With local flowers, people get a good value for what they're buying," Kevin says. "My costs may be as high as somebody who is shipping flowers from Costa Rica, but because I'm local, I actually have a better quality flower product to sell."

## Best dahlias for the cutting garden and vase

The flowers of most garden dahlias are suitable for cutting; however, some are better than others, says Kevin who mentions eye appeal, bloom yield, bloom substance, stem length and stem strength as preferred characteristics. "Together, these traits make the difference between a bouquet that lasts three days versus one that will last a week."

Corralitos Gardens list favorite cut-dahlia workhorses on its web site (see resources, page 141). In general, look for blooms classified as poms, balls, and informal or formal decorative – all of which tend to hold together and last longer in the vase. Unlike some flowers, which can be cut when in bud and allowed to gradually open wider in water, the bloom on a dahlia remains at the same stage as when it was cut – another good reason to harvest your flowers or buy them from a farmer as close as possible to when you want to use them.

**Above, from top:** Unlike factory-grown flowers that never see the light of day or have their roots touch soil, Kevin and Karen's dahlias are part of a balanced ecosystem – bugs included; Kevin singles out a melon-hued, ball-shaped dahlia to demonstrate the type of bloom that lasts best as a cut flower.

# SUBLIME AND SENSUOUS

## By design, a Sunday brunch that's a feast for the eyes

Designer **Melissa Feveyear** appreciates the traditional definition of a florist: "It used to be a person who grew and sold their own flowers," she explains. By choosing and gathering botanical ingredients inspired by that old-fashioned notion, the Seattle florist considers flowers from a grower's point of view, asking *"Where was it grown?" "How was it cultivated?"* and *"When does it reach peak beauty in the vase?"*

Yet, instead of owning rural acreage planted with romantic rows of annuals and perennials, Melissa is firmly planted on city soil at Terra Bella Organic Floral & Botanical Designs, a 1,000-square-foot flower shop in Seattle's Greenwood neighborhood. Curiosity and intentionality are two of her design tools; she selects foliage, blooms, and other fresh-from-the-field elements with the same care as if she personally grew each ephemeral blossom or stem in her own backyard. That connection with nature is vitally important to her artistic philosophy.

"If flowers aren't locally or organically grown, then they are most likely coming from some huge factory farm," she says. "My customers do not want flowers dipped in strong pesticides on their dinner table."

Most of the flowers in Terra Bella's designs are sustainably grown or Veriflora Certified. A segment of commercially-grown flowers bears this designation, but Melissa isn't wedded to labeling. Instead, she hungers for uncommon blooms – the type of flower not likely to show up at the wholesale market. She's become a flower sleuth, tapping into unique, hard-to-find botanical sources. This means raiding her private garden and the backyards of family and friends, developing relationships with local, organic flower farms, and looking for specialty growers whose crops aren't durable enough to ship long distances.

With a sweetheart face framed by cascading red tendrils, Melissa's appearance is as old-fashioned and dreamy as the blooms she designs. Similarly, her floral inspiration comes from the past and the present-day.

When we asked Melissa to design flowers for an elegant Sunday brunch – in the dead of winter – she responded with amazing creativity and fashioned one arrangement for the

**Above:** Melissa Feveyear, owner of Terra Bella Organic Floral & Botanical Designs in Seattle, sources her ingredients from local flower farmers and foragers like Tosh Rosford.

**Opposite:** Evoking the flowers immortalized on the canvases of Old-World painters, Melissa created a rich, botanical palette of blooms, foliage, fruit and branches. The bouquet's ingredients come from local, sustainable farms and private gardens.

buffet table and a corresponding spray of blooms for the fireplace mantel. The setting's chocolate-burgundy-cream-and-teal color scheme, vintage furnishings and heirloom china and serving pieces presented a romantic backdrop for Melissa's floral palette. "I picked out a selection of apricot, cool orange, and ruby-red flowers that together make a beautiful, juicy bouquet," Melissa explains. "I opted for this combination, simply because these are the colors that inspire me."

She selected a vintage 36-inch glass vase for the main event. Fluted at the rim and base, its sensuous lines were well-suited for the unstructured but sophisticated presentation Melissa had in mind. Gracing the mantel, a verdigris cachepot contained a similarly copious arrangement using many of the same flowers and greenery.

This event took place in January, when many floral designers find it hard to locate seasonal and locally-grown ingredients. Yet Melissa had a surprisingly bountiful selection from which to choose. Garden-fresh foliage provided the foundation for her design, including shiny acanthus leaves from Jello Mold Farms. Other greenery included boughs of heavenly bamboo *(Nandina domestica)*, glossy-leaved camellia branches and dagger ferns – all clipped from private gardens.

Melissa's evocative designs could easily be mistaken for still-life arrangements associated with the Dutch masters of the early 17th century. Luscious and ruffled, saffron-and-crimson parrot tulips were central to her vision. Amethyst-colored hyacinths promised springtime with their intoxicating scent. Apricot, coral and plum-red roses – including those grown sustainably in Oregon and Ecuador – infused the bouquet with romance, while bud-laden branches of coral quince and white-flowering forsythia lent texture and seasonal interest. And, just like the Dutch painters, Melissa invited the orchard's bounty into her arrangement with sliced pomegranates and fuzzy apricots.

The completed designs conjured an Old-World narrative in which each flower conveyed a symbolic message to anyone who witnessed its beauty.

**Above, from top:** Even during January in Seattle, a floral designer like Melissa can realize her creative vision thanks to a rainbow of sustainable tulips, grown by Alm Hill Gardens in Everson, Washington; Tosh supplies Melissa and other designers with wild-harvested and cultivated floral elements, including Japanese fantail willow (*Salix udensis* 'Sekka'), with an unusual, contorted form.

## The Organic Question

For the Sunday brunch bouquet, Melissa originally envisioned using voluptuous garden roses. She asked a sustainable farmer from Oregon to deliver flowers in her desired peachy-apricot palette. (In the Northwest, even during chilly winters, a few growers raise flowers in protected greenhouses to satisfy year-round demand.)

"When the roses arrived, though, they didn't have the look and feel I had hoped for, nor were they quite the right color," she says. This unexpected, day-of-the-party-mishap is something designers face all the time, but it creates a special challenge for florists committed to using only seasonal and locally-sourced ingredients. As a result, Melissa supplemented the original rose palette with 'Milva', a pretty soft apricot rose imported from a sustainable farm in Ecuador. "I had to change my vision for the design to use different flowers that were available but also in keeping with my values," she explains.

Fortunately, the dark plum-red spray roses and spicy orange hybrid tea roses from Peterkort Roses, the Oregon grower, were gorgeous, lending a nice contrast to the design's softer botanical elements.

Like *locavores* who want their food to originate within a 100-mile radius, eco-savvy floral designers have their own definition of "local" when sourcing botanical material. Melissa's challenge is to balance her desire for organically-grown blooms with the environmental impact of ordering cut flowers from

**Above:** Designing with sustainably-grown flowers is important to Melissa, who is concerned about exposure to pesticides used in conventional flower crops.

domestic and international growers beyond her corner of the U.S. These artistic and ethical decisions are reflected in each one of her beautiful bouquets.

In fact, Terra Bella influences the entire chain of people with whom it comes into contact, since Melissa seeks out and supports farmers with a compatible philosophy about flower-growing. She strives to encourage and educate her customers about the many benefits of requesting "green" flowers. "My customers do care about supporting the community and local farmers. But they don't always think about how organic flowers will affect them personally. That is, until they learn how many pesticides are in conventionally-grown cut flowers. That awareness is only just starting."

### Eco-Tip

"Oasis," is a Styrofoam-like product made from petrochemicals. While florists have for years used the generic green blocks of foam to stabilize stems in low or wide-mouthed vases, Melissa doesn't want to expose herself, her clients, or the environment to the material. Research for a healthier, organic substitute led her to wood aspen. Also known as excelsior, the material is comprised of fine wood fibers. It is often used as packaging material for wine bottles and other break-ables. "It isn't treated with chemicals like florist foam and it doesn't degrade quickly in water," Melissa says. Stems and branches can be inserted into the tangle of natural-colored wood aspen inside a vase. Excelsior is available at craft shops and from online sources that sell packaging material.

### Design Technique

Melissa creates romantic, sophisticated bouquets by designing with a light hand. She highlights the natural form and shape of each flower, stem and branch by letting them fall gently into place (rather than manipulating or contorting them). One of her favorite techniques is to group similar blooms together as they would appear in the garden. "I like to cluster flowers," she says. These pleasing groupings give Melissa's bouquets added interest and make her designs feel "just picked."

## Floral Ingredients

**Seasonal and sustainably-grown**
Parrot tulips and hyacinths,
Alm Hill Gardens, Bellingham, WA

Acanthus leaves, flowering quince
branches and white forsythia
(*Abeliophyllum distichum*),
Jello Mold Farm, Mt. Vernon, WA

Heavenly bamboo (*Nandina domestica*),
Jean Zaputil's garden, Seattle

Western sword fern
(*Polystichum munitum*),
Jean Fiala's garden, Fall City, WA

Camellia branches,
Melissa Feveyear's garden, Seattle

**Wild-foraged ingredients**
*Pieris japonica,* from "Tosh," a Seattle hunter-gatherer who gleans natural ingredients and sells them to floral designers

**Locally-grown ingredients**
Spray roses, garden roses and maiden fern,
Peterkort Roses, Oregon

**Eco-Certified flowers**
'Milva' roses, Ecuador

**Above:** Tosh's offerings come straight from the woods, meadows or fields. Floral designers rely on this hunter-gatherer for the types of branches and stems (including this colorful twig dogwood) that give their arrangements a naturalistic look.

**Left:** Melissa relies on relationships with local flower farmers who specialize in unique, sustainably-grown crops. She frequently shops for flowers at Seattle's Pike Place Market, where Alm Hill Gardens sells field-grown tulips almost every month of the year. Here, Alm Hill's Mejken Poore wraps tulips for sale to customers.

**Opposite:** A sublime spectrum of coral, apricot and red roses inspired the Sunday brunch bouquet. Jean Zaputil, a Seattle artist, garden and interior designer, styled the floral portrait, including the lavish tabletop spread photographed at Terra Bella.

# FLOWERS FOR CHEZ PANISSE

**Nothing but seasonal, locally-grown flowers decorate the Berkeley, California, bistro that boldly launched the modern farm-to-table movement 40 years ago**

A serendipitous conversation with Flora Grubb led us to the legendary Chez Panisse Cafe & Restaurant, home of Alice Waters' inspiring, community-minded culinary endeavors. As we wrapped up an interview and photography at Flora's stylish flower and garden shop in San Francisco, she said in a completely off-handed manner, "I want to introduce you to my friend **Max Gill**. He does the flowers for Chez Panisse. Do you want to meet him?"

Our answer was an unequivocal "Yes," and so Flora made that call.

Three days later, we found ourselves in the heart of Berkeley, standing on the porch of a gracefully aging, century-old Craftsman bungalow. Max opened the door, greeted us warmly and suggested we follow him on a tour of his backyard, a.k.a. the cutting garden. With David clicking away like he was on a high-fashion shoot, the three of us moved comfortably from polite chitchat to passionate story-swapping as we discovered our mutual obsession for gardening, unusual ornamental plants and local floral design ingredients – cultivated or foraged.

"I like to work with what's local and sustainable, but also what you'd see growing together in nature," says the handsome young designer with a big following. For him the term "local" means sourcing flowers from Bay Area farms, as well as "from someone down the street who has a crabapple tree." Twice each week Max creates fresh arrangements for Chez Panisse.

Inside the intimate restaurant, small cafe tabletops barely accommodate dishes and cutlery, let alone something like a bud vase. As a result, foodies who clamor for a seat at the popular $60-$95 prix fixe dinners are treated to Max's dramatic arrangements displayed elsewhere throughout Chez Panisse. One huge urn graces an entry table and another is situated in an alcove between two seating areas. Upstairs in the Chez Panisse Cafe, where things are more casual, Max adds vases of hand-gathered blooms, vines, and foliage on the kitchen ledge.

Whether he uses berry-laden hawthorn branches or delicate clematis vines, Max feels privileged to design bouquets that are as local and seasonal as Chez Panisse's menus. His client, Alice Waters, has this to say about the designer: "Max is an amazing forager – he brings a sense of aliveness and seasonality, reinforcing the principles of the restaurant."

With an intense gaze that focuses on his subject, be it a human being or the raw material with which he works, Max could be easily mistaken for an actor or model. An eclectic background informs his aesthetic, including a University of California at Berkeley degree in environmental science and city planning. Max has supported himself as a massage therapist, dog-walker, bartender and – yes, a theatrical actor and print model. In 2003, through a bartending gig at the restaurant next to Chez Panisse, he learned of an opening with Chez Panisse's floral designer Carrie Glenn. At the time, Max Gill Design, his small floral studio, relied on word-of-mouth referrals and freelance work with other designers, including Ariella Chezar,

**Above:** An effortless urn-filled bouquet, created by Max Gill, adorns the counter at the upstairs Chez Panisse Cafe. To the left of the arrangement is a stack of Alice Waters' many bestselling cookbooks.

**Opposite:** On location prior to the dinner opening, Max works as adroitly as the chefs seen cooking in Chez Panisse's kitchen behind him. He uses seasonal and sustainably-grown floral ingredients, including those harvested from his own nearby backyard.

a successful floral artist who has since relocated to Massachusetts. "It was pretty grass roots – I was designing in Mason jars and cutting stuff under the freeway," he jokes.

Max says that the assisting position with the woman who had defined Chez Panisse's decor since it opened in 1971, was a three-year apprenticeship. The experience introduced him to many new approaches, such as using live plants. "Carrie showed me that it is as important to go to a nursery to buy a 5-gallon plant as it is to head to the flower market," he says. "She is responsible for the whole genre of field-to-vase flowers. I've often wondered who she's the reincarnation of, because she's brilliant and working with her pushed all my aesthetic buttons."

By 2007, having assumed the position as Chez Panisse's floral designer upon Carrie's retirement, Max decided to "go for it" and expand his business. A bank loan helped fund renovations to an elderly one-car garage adjacent to his house in Berkeley, where, incidentally, Max grew up. A new concrete slab floor, corrugated metal roof, cottage-style windows, power and water have turned the structure into an attractive and functional design studio. It's here that Max preps and produces flowers for his private wedding and event clients, as well as Chez Panisse, which is located a few blocks away. Behind his studio is the cutting garden, where Max grows many of his own botanical ingredients. "I lean on the garden pretty heavily, especially in the summer," Max says of the perennial beds, woody shrubs and countless clematis vines that occupy most of the 7,000-square-foot city lot.

He hopes his field-to-vase sensibility resonates with diners who appreciate Chez Panisse's farm-to-table approach. While Alice Waters has nurtured an entire cottage industry of organic food purveyors, her floral designer similarly encourages his suppliers. If it's not grown in his own backyard, Max turns to people like Vicki and Valerie Prosek, sisters who are partners in Florist @ Large. "They have relationships with farmers that no one else has," Max enthuses. "If I want fruiting branches, I call them."

The association with Chez Panisse allows Max to support and educate local growers. "Many have been around for generations and, no, maybe some of them haven't jumped on the organic bandwagon yet. Some local flowers are conventionally grown. But education goes a long way. I find myself asking them: 'What did you grow that you *did not* have to spray?' And by making it really clear where my dollar will go, I feel strongly that I'm including everybody in the 'sustainable' conversation."

## Feeding the eyes of diners

We followed Max's car to Chez Panisse, located at 1517 Shattuck Ave., in Berkeley. He brought along some yummy coral-colored dahlias to refresh a naturalistic composition on display in the main dining room. "I have to credit Alice Waters for making this possible," Max declares, sweeping his arms wide. "My goal is to make it feel like all these rustic elements are growing together – that they literally grew here."

Admittedly, he calls his designs "high maintenance, since I don't always use elements that last on their own for a whole week without refreshing." Max is more than hands-on, stopping by Chez Panisse almost daily to refresh the water in vases or replace a tired bloom. "Let's face it, ingredients last longer if you can cut them in your own garden," he points out. "When I cut dahlias from my backyard, I get three or four more days out of each flower than the ones from the flower market."

**Above:** A stunning floral display is perched on a ledge separating two dining sections of the Arts and Crafts-era restaurant. Max incorporated locally-grown dahlias, branches and vines in this seasonal arrangement.

Drawing from his theatre background, Max composes each arrangement "as a little stage," similar to a classical theatre set based on a grid design. "Each area of the stage has its own significance, such as the upper-left stage corner – a very powerful position where people always look to first," he says. Similarly, Max places eye-catching focal ingredients in the upper-left area of his arrangement. "The front-center area of a stage is a really intimate place, where an actor might confess a detail to the audience. In a floral arrangement, that center front spot is an opportunity to place something a little sweet or personal, like a tiny tendril reaching down to the table." In designing flowers using theatrical principles that have been around for millennia, Max creates a visual story that flows from beginning to end.

Of Max, his design mentor Ariella Chezar proclaimed: "Max, with his heart of gold, is a genius at creating small, magical worlds that you cannot help but be drawn into. With tenderness and skill, he assembles his elements, resulting in the most perfect balance of haphazard wildness and clear purpose. His arrangements *always* look just right."

As a one-man studio who often relies on other freelance designers to assist him, Max feels that his own aesthetic is constantly evolving. "Having been fortunate enough to work with people like Carrie Glenn and Ariella Chezar – people who have very big shoes to fill – I know I'm still exploring my own design style. I want to realize and create for people their vision for their special day," he explains. "I can't stress how grateful I feel to be able to do that."

# Flower & Foliage Resources

*"I don't see anybody getting out of flower farming – and that's amazing to me. It is an extremely addictive career. I don't want to minimize how much work is involved, but once you've grown flowers, it's hard to quit."*

**– Lynn Byczynski,**
author, publisher, flower farmer

# From Their Fields to Your Vase

**For nearly 25 years, the passionate members of the Association of Specialty Cut Flower Growers have shared knowledge and ideas with each other – with the goal of creating successful domestic cut flower farmers**

After more than a decade of decline, America's cut flower production is on the rise, with significant increases every year. Recent data from the U.S. Department of Agriculture showed California as the top-producing state, with a wholesale value of $286 million, accounting for 76 percent of all cut flowers grown in the country. Washington State's flower fields followed at $22 million in cut flowers. New Jersey produced nearly $12.5 million and Oregon $10 million.

These numbers are impressive. That is, until you learn that imports account for 80 percent of all cut flowers sold in the U.S. But with everyone from brides to party hosts asking for better selection and quality from the blooms they purchase, the local farmer is responding in turn, planting more exciting varieties each season. Even the explosion of farmers' markets across the country underscores the "buy local" consumer movement. According to the USDA, there were 7,175 farmers' markets operating across the country in 2010, up 17% over the previous year. This trend shows no signs of slowing.

Some of the optimism we and others are feeling about the future of the local flower movement is fueled by anecdotal evidence. Jay White, a writer for *Texas Gardener* magazine, proclaimed in a recent article that "locally grown, fresh cut flowers are the fastest growing segment of the U.S. floral market."

I ran his statement by Lynn Byczynski, publisher for the past 20 years of *Growing for Market,* a national magazine serving market growers of both edible and ornamental crops, and a veteran cut flower farmer whose Lawrence, Kansas-based Wild Onion Farm produces a bounty of annuals and perennials for its local floral industry.

"Those figures are hard to quantify because the USDA doesn't capture all of the small local growers who aren't showing up in the statistics," Lynn explains. "But you know, I don't see anybody getting out of flower farming – and that's amazing to me. It is an extremely addictive career. I don't want to minimize how much work is involved, but once you've grown flowers, it's hard to quit."

## A community of flower growers

The Association of Specialty Cut Flower Growers is a critical "hub" for anyone involved in growing flowers commercially. The organization has 600 members across the U.S. and in several other countries, and it publishes *The Cut Flower Quarterly.* ASCFG also awards research grants and conducts seed trials, funding independent growers who conduct on-farm research and academics who conduct university trials.

The organization's roots can be traced to a 1987 "Field Grown Cut Flowers" conference hosted by Dr. Allan Armitage, horticulture professor at the University of Georgia at Athens, and his then-research technician Judy Marriott Laushman. To accommodate ongoing requests from those interested in touring their cut flower trials, they staged a two-day event, attracting cut flower growers, seed companies, cooperative extension agents and suppliers from around the country.

"We expected about 50 people from the Southeast to show up," recalls Judy, now the ASCFG executive director. "We would have been thrilled to have 75, but the final count drew 163 attendees. We were more than thrilled – we were shocked."

Without any big plan, the small idea mushroomed into a veritable movement. "It was a special time because the conference let people who were toiling away in anonymity meet others just like them," Allan recalls. Judy produced "The Georgia Report," the first publication of its kind to address growing cut flowers. And many of those who attended asked for more. One of the speakers suggested the need for a new growers association that could serve as a clearinghouse for grass-roots and research-based information alike.

"The idea just didn't die," Judy says. In 1988, thirty people attended the first organizational meeting of the "National Field Cut Flower Growers Association." Later renamed the ASCFG, the association is the sole industry source focused on both the science and art of cut flower farming. And as one of its instigators, Allan couldn't be more pleased. "I loved sitting back and watching this small gem of an idea turn into a diamond pendant. And I'm still in awe that an organization like this evolved from a few beds of flowers."

**Above:** Early in the season, Andy Kirkpatrick plants perennial floral crops at Jello Mold Farm in Mount Vernon, Washington.

**Opposite:** Mary Dean operates Buena Vista Flowers in Oregon's Willamette Valley. A grower and floral designer, she regularly sells her inventive bouquets at the Salem Saturday Market, drawing from the hundreds of botanical varieties she raises each year. Mary is a new member of ASCFG, who had farmed without camaraderie for years and then joined the group of like-minded people.

**Previous spread:** A farm cart brims with intoxicating bunches of lilacs grown by ASCFG member Ed Pincus of Third Branch Flower, a Roxbury, Vermont, farm. Ed and his family have produced and sold their irresistible field-grown flowers to the wholesale market since 1987.

## Open source

ASCFG focuses on education and information sharing. The Bulletin Board, a members' online chat room, connects growers all over North America. Some of the discussions are specific, such as whether and when to dig dahlia bulbs or what is the best material for installing a hoop house.

And other voices express more philosophical or personal concerns, such as a recent question from Emily Watson, of Milwaukee, Wisconsin-based Stems Cut Flowers. She wrote:

*"I've been growing for less than five years, on a small plot, and I'm wondering if this is a good idea. I'm not looking to get rich overnight, or even at all. But I need to pay the bills, maybe support a family and retire some day (before I'm 90). I do not have a problem working a few 80-hour weeks but I do not want that to be the norm. Am I crazy for thinking this? The bottom line is I need to know if this is possible before I sink any more money into it?"*

The responses Emily received were encouraging and honest; no one tried to sugarcoat the truth about the backbreaking reality of running a small farm. They also revealed that people do not grow and market flowers because it's lucrative, but at least in part for a love of the land and a passion for the independent lifestyle it brings.

*"I have been able to make a frugal living by growing cut flowers for 20 years, with no outside income or partner with an income,"* wrote Nellie Gardner from Flower Fields, of Rochester, N.Y. *"I can only do it by working like a madwoman most of the year, doing weddings, developing many outlets, and extending my Zone 5 season by making Christmas wreaths [and] offering workshops and classes. To make a living with cut flowers, you not only have to grow efficiently, have quality [product], sell to florists, wedding and special event designers, and sell in both retail and wholesale channels, you also have to reinvent yourself to sell all your skills to the public who is hungry for anything real. The competition is cheap labor in South America and the use of flowers as loss leaders in stores like Sam's Club and BJ's. Only some consumers will buy on conscience, not price."*

**Above:** The ASCFG's elder statesman, Joseph Schmitt of Fair Field Flowers in Madison, Wisconsin, is a third generation flower farmer and frequent instructor at regional and national Growers' Schools.

Diane Szukovathy, from Jello Mold Farm in the Pacific Northwest, voiced her wish for more advocacy, among other things:

*"There is a resilient movement in this country to buy local and support local farmers – and we hold the quality card,"* she wrote. *"Still, cheap imports have taken their toll on [domestic] flower farmers. In my opinion, not enough has been done to promote public awareness of the state of our industry. It's a cynical state of affairs; but most of those who are wealthy in the cut flower industry in this country make their money from mark-ups on cheap imports. A well-organized, strategic marketing campaign might make the difference between scraping by and thriving for the flower farmers who want to make a living in this country from farming. Certainly, that is part of the experiment we are conducting with the Seattle Wholesale Growers Market Cooperative."*

**Above:** Young flower farmer Jessica Gring works for Jello Mold Farm several days each week. She is an eager sponge who soaks up the wisdom and ideas of more experienced growers while planning to start her own small venture in the future.

Longtime Oskaloosa, Iowa-based flower farmer Quinton Tschetter added a more personal reminder:

*". . . don't forget the sheer benefit to the individual in exercise and satisfaction in growing those beautiful flowers, the connections with customers and other intangibles that one encounters as time goes by. Oh, the love of the job!"*

It's inspiring to watch established flower farmers coach the next generation of grower – all with the goal of sustaining a healthy domestic cut flower industry.

"ASCFG is a really unusual trade organization," Lynn Byczynski says. "I see little in the way of professional rivalry. There is such a culture of mentoring that you don't always find in other groups. Where else can you find people who are as passionate about flowers as you are?"

# Floral Glossary

**Above:** Fragrant sweet peas evoke an impossible-to-ignore sensory response. When harvested in clusters and arranged in buckets, the mix of petal colors is impressive.

**Opposite, bottom:** With the right connections between farmer and floral designer, it's possible to enjoy an abundance of organically-grown tulips and other flowering bulbs, even in the off-season. These intensely-hued tulips offer designers a versatile floral palette with which to work.

## Basic elements of a floral arrangement:

**Foliage or greenery:** One way to stabilize the more prominent flowers in a vase is to begin with foliage, arranging the stems so they create a grid-like framework under water. Foliage textures fill the vase opening and stabilize the flower stems that will be added later. You can also use vintage flower frogs or a loosely-formed piece of chicken wire hidden inside the vase to stabilize foliage and flower stems. These eco-friendly tools can be used over and over again.

**Diva or focal flowers:** These blooms are the leading stars of a bouquet. Look for flowers that the eye reads as a distinct shape or form. Many designers prefer to work with uneven numbers (3 or 5, depending on the size of the vase) – and the arrangement usually looks more appealing if the stem lengths are varied.

**Line or vertical ingredients:** Linear elements can be created with flowers, branches or foliage. They serve as an arrangement's "exclamation point" to add contrast to the more dominant diva flowers.

**Secondary or filler ingredients:** Like embellishing a garment with embroidery, these are the lacy and ruffled elements of an arrangement. Use tiny, ethereal annuals, perennials or herbs as "filler" in the gaps and spaces between the diva flowers.

**Spiller or collar ingredients:** Flowers, vines and foliage can visually connect the overall floral arrangement with the vase or vessel. Spiller ingredients drape and cascade over the rim of the vase. Collar ingredients resemble a "ruff" that encircles the vase's opening and gives the arrangement a tailored, finished look.

## Color rules:

**Tonal or monochromatic:** A single hue, or variations of a color. One way to strengthen a monochromatic-themed design is with colored foliage – such as using gold, silver, lime or burgundy rather than just greenery to echo the flower palette.

**Contrast:** Color "pairs" that reside opposite each other on the classic artist's color wheel. Some options include: red and green (in the plant world, this can be slightly reinterpreted, such as maroon flowers with blue-green foliage); or yellow and purple; or blue and orange.

**Analogous:** Flowers representing adjacent colors on the color wheel. Red-yellow-orange are analogous colors; similarly, blue-green-violet colors are analogous. Remember that the vase color can also play a role in this scheme.

## Care tips:

1. Always use fresh, room-temperature or slightly cooler water in a clean vessel.

2. Cut flower, foliage and other stems with clean floral shears or a sharp knife. Cut at a 45-degree angle to increase the surface area that will "drink" vase water.

3. Remove foliage from the portion of the stem that will be under water.

4. Display the vase in a cool area away from direct sunlight. To refresh and extend the life of your flowers, change the water every day or two, re-cut the stems (1/4-inch to 1/2-inch from the bottom) and remove random spoiled stems.

**Above:** A garden bouquet picked and held by photographer David Perry contains vermillion-red *Photinia sp.* with contrasting greens – hellebore flowers and carex blades.

## Seasonal Gifts

During each month of the year the garden has something wonderful to offer floral designers. Enhance your cut flower arrangements with ingredients harvested from your own backyard, the flowers grown and sold by farmers' market vendors and even the "weeds" gleaned from wild places. Here are some of the ingredients you will find, season by season, depending on where you live.

**Above:** Late-season persimmons, which are valued as an ornamental element in autumn arrangements.

## WINTER

**December:**

**Branches:** beautyberry (*Callicarpa bodinieri*), ilex (with berries), twig dogwoods, snowberry

**Bulbs:** amaryllis, paper whites

**Greenery/foliage:** acanthus, cardoon, Camellia sasanqua, Dusty Miller, evergreen boughs, holly, *Magnolia grandiflora*, rosemary

**Potted plants:** cattleya orchids

**January:**

**Branches:** birch, filbert (contorted and standard), willow (curly and colored, witch hazel)

**Bulbs:** amaryllis, snowdrops

**Fruit:** citrus (kumquat, lemons, limes) on the branch

**Greenery/foliage:** pieris, sweet box (*Sarcococca*), white forsythia (*Abeliophyllum distichum*)

**Potted plants:** lady slipper orchids

**February:**

**Branches:** forsythia, paper bush (*Edgeworthia chrysantha*), pussy willow, quince, winter hazel (*Corylopsis spicata*), wintersweet (*Chimonanthus praecox*), *Stachyurus praecox*

**Bulbs:** crocus, snowflake (*Leucojum aestivum*)

**Greenery/foliage:** cardoon, eleagnus, Mexican orange (*Choisya ternata*), winter daphne (*Daphne odora*)

**Potted plants:** cymbidium orchids

## SPRING

**March:**

**Branches/flowering shrubs:** deutzia, quince, flowering plum

**Bulbs:** daffodils, iris, ranunculus

**Flowers:** anemones, artichoke, pinks (*Dianthus*), hellebores (*Helleborus foetidus, H. argutifolius, H. orientalis*), Icelandic poppies, Italian bugloss (*Anchusa azurea*), lupine, money plant (*Lunaria annua*), wallflowers

**Greenery/foliage:** euphorbia (*Euphorbia robbiae* or *E.* 'Fireglow'), lady's mantle, rosemary, ninebark

**April:**

**Branches/flowering shrubs:** lilacs, viburnum (*Viburnum* x *burkwoodii*)

**Bulbs:** bluebells, hyacinth, fritillaria, grape hyacinth (*Muscari*), ranunculus, tulips

**Flowers:** bleeding heart, hellebores (*Helleborus orientalis*), Icelandic poppies

**Greenery/foliage:** box, heuchera, spiraea

**May:**

**Bulbs:** allium, foxtail lily (*Eremurus*), lily of the valley, parrot tulips

**Flowers:** campanula, columbine, foxglove, lupine, nasturtium, peonies (tree and herbaceous)

**Flowering shrubs:** snowball viburnum, mock orange, flowering dogwood

**Greenery/foliage:** pittosporum

**Vines:** passiflora

## SUMMER

**June:**

**Bulbs:** allium, calla lilies, trumpet lilies

**Flowers:** astilbe, burnet (Sanguisorba), calendula, delphinium, Helenium, nigella, phlox, Queen Anne's lace, scabiosa, sweet peas, yarrow

**Flowering shrubs:** garden roses

**Foliage:** herbs, lamb's ear, hosta, ornamental grasses, scented pelargonium, succulents

**Fruit:** alpine strawberries, unripe orchard fruit (apples, plums, peaches) on the branch, unripe raspberries or blackberries on the vine

**July:**

**Bulbs:** butterfly gladiolas, calla lilies, oriental lilies

**Flowers:** perennials (every variety), cerinthe, delphinium, echinops, Joe Pye weed (Eupatorium), lisianthus, monkshood, rudbeckia, snapdragons

**Flowering shrubs:** garden roses, lavender

**Foliage:** artemisia, geranium, ornamental oregano

**Fruit:** figs (fruit and foliage)

**Vines:** clematis, grape, jasmine

**August:**

**Bulbs:** tuberoses

**Flowering shrubs:** hydrangeas

**Flowers:** agapanthus, celosia, sunflowers, zinnias

**Foliage:** baptisia, cardoon, rubus

**Fruit/vegetables:** currant tomatoes

## FALL

**September:**

**Flowering shrubs:** 'antique' hydrangeas, asters, beautyberry, chestnut, currant, smoke bush, viburnum

**Flowers:** amaranth, bluebeard (Caryopteris), chocolate cosmos, dahlias, helenium, hypericum, monkshood

**Foliage:** ornamental grasses

**Fruit/vegetables:** ornamental peppers, pomegranate

**Vines:** hops, sweet autumn clematis

**October:**

**Bulbs:** nerine

**Flowering shrubs:** crabapple, rose hips, snowberry

**Flowers:** Chinese lanterns, helenium, mums

**Foliage:** broom corn, fall leaves on the branch, ornamental grasses

**Vines:** bittersweet

**Fruit/vegetables:** heirloom squash, gourds, pumpkins (fruit, vines, foliage)

**November:**

**Branches/flowering shrubs:** coralberry (Symphoricarpos), crabapple, rose hips, roses (domestically-grown or fair-trade imported), snowberry, twig dogwood

**Flowers:** mums

**Foliage:** viburnum, weigela

**Fruit/vegetables:** heirloom apples on the branch, flowering cabbage, kale

**Above, from top:** Lilacs, like these indigo-purple heirloom blooms, are synonymous with early summer. Cut from the garden and paired with wispy tendrils of golden hops (Humulus lupulus 'Aureus'), the bouquet is hugely appealing; the vintage aqua blue canning jar serves as a lovely vessel for a springtime bunch of hybrid daffodils (Narcissus cyclamineus 'Jet Fire').

# Sustainability Terms

The terminology and definitions used in this book – and in the flower industry – are used by state and federal certification agencies, as well as by numerous third-party certification organizations. Here is a list of those terms:

**Biodynamics:** Considered a holistic method of agriculture, the term is based on a philosophy that all aspects of the farm should be treated as an interrelated whole. ❖

**California Certified Organic:** California Certified Organic Farmers (CCOF) has been certifying products as organic since 1973 and is accredited by the USDA. Only products containing at least 95% organic ingredients may display the USDA Organic seal in addition to the certifier's logo. ▲

**Certified Organic:** Used to describe an item grown according to strict uniform standards verified by independent state or private organizations. ✿

**CSA:** An abbreviation for Community Supported Agriculture, CSA is a system in which consumers support a local farm by paying in advance for agricultural products. This reduces the financial risks for the farmer because the costs of seeds and planting crops are covered in advance by consumers. ❖

**Fair Trade Certified:** To bear this label, products must be grown by small-scale producers democratically organized in either cooperatives or unions. In order to use the Fair Trade Certified label, the buyer must also be willing to pay up to 60% of the purchase in advance for some products, with added premiums for social development projects, including healthcare, educational and capacity-building projects that can improve quality of life for farming communities. ✿

**IPM:** Integrated Pest Management (IPM) refers to various methods of natural pest control, such as habitat manipulation, biological control, and pest-resistant plants. Pesticides are used in the smallest possible amounts only when other techniques prove inadequate. ❖

**Local:** As is the case with the term "sustainable," there are numerous definitions of "local." In 2008 Congress passed H.R. 2419, which amended the "Consolidated Farm and Rural Development Act." In the amendment, "locally" and "regionally" are grouped together and are defined as:

  (I) the locality or region in which the final product is marketed, so that the total distance that the product is transported is less than 400 miles from the origin of the product; or (II) the State in which the product is produced. – Bill Text - 110th Congress (2007-2008) - THOMAS (Library of Congress)

In May 2010 the USDA acknowledged this definition in an informational leaflet. Those who prefer to eat locally grown/produced food sometimes call themselves *locavores.* ◆

**Organic:** According to a definition adopted by the National Organic Standards Board in 1997, "organic agriculture" is an ecological production management system that promotes and enhances biodiversity, biological cycles and soil biological activity. ✿

**Salmon Safe:** A program that recognizes farm and other land use operations that contribute to restoring stream eco-system health in important native salmon fisheries of the Pacific Northwest. ❖

**Sustainable:** A product can be considered sustainable if its production enables the resources from which it was made to continue to be available for future generations. The drawback of the term 'sustainable' is that it lacks a clear-cut, universally-accepted, enforceable definition – thus it can be interpreted in different ways. It is more of a philosophy or way of life than a label. ❖

**Veriflora:** An agricultural sustainability certification and eco-labeling program recognized in the floriculture and horticulture industries. ★

Quoted and referenced sources:

✿ The Organic Trade Association (www.ota.com)

❖ Sustainable Table (www.sustainabletable.org/intro/dictionary/)

▲ Green Choices/Consumer Reports (www.greenerchoices.org)

❖ Salmon Safe (www.salmonsafe.org)

◆ USDA: (www.ers.usda.gov/Publications/ERR97/ERR97_ReportSummary.pdf)

★ Veriflora (www.veriflora.com)

# Resources

Here is the contact information for the many farms, studios and individuals featured in *The 50 Mile Bouquet*. VIDEO BONUS: look for this symbol **"V"** indicating a corresponding video at our web site, **www.the50milebouquet.com.**

**AUTHOR/PHOTOGRAPHER CONTACTS:**
Debra Prinzing, **www.debraprinzing.com**
David E. Perry, **www.davidperryphoto.com**

**FOREWORD (PAGE 9)**
Amy Stewart, **www.amystewart.com**

**INTRODUCTION (PAGES 10-15)**
California Cut Flower Commission, 916-441-1701; **www.ccfc.org**
Love 'n Fresh Flowers; **www.lovenfreshflowers.com**

**CHAPTER 1 (PAGES 16-57)**
**With Love, from Skagit Valley**
Jello Mold Farm, 206-290-3154; **www.jellomoldfarm.com**

**Brimming with Blooms**
Seattle Wholesale Growers Market, 206-838-1523;
**www.seattlewholesalegrowersmarket.com**

J. Foss Garden Flowers; **www.jfossgardenflowers.com**

Oregon Coastal Flowers, 888-815-0885; **www.flowersbulbs.com**

Everyday Flowers; **everydayflowers@live.com**

**The Last Rose Farm in Oregon**
Peterkort Roses, 503-628-1005; **www.peterkortroses.com**

**Mail-Order Organic**
California Organic Flowers, 530-891-6265;
**www.californiaorganicflowers.com**

**Rocky Mountain Bouquet**
The Fresh Herb Co., 303-449-5994; **www.thefreshherbco.com**

**Flower Patch Politics**
Silver Lake Farms, 323-644-3700; **www.silverlakefarms.com**

**Grower Wisdom**
Le Mera Gardens, 541-857-8223; **www.lemeragardens.com (V)**

Choice Bulb Co., 360-424-4685; **www.choicebulb.com (V)**

Alm Hill Gardens; **www.growingwashington.org**

Charles Little & Co.; **charleslittle@comcast.net (V)**

**CHAPTER 2 (PAGES 58-87)**
**The Accidental Flower Farmer**
Lila B. Flowers, Gardens and Events, 415-563-6681;
**www.lilabdesign.com**

**The Cutting Garden**
The Cutting Garden at Flora Grubb Gardens, 415-626-7256;
**www.floragrubb.com (V)**

**The Green Bouquet**
Blush Custom Floral, 206-972-1840; **www.blushcustomfloral.com**

**Tradition with a Twist**
Babylon Floral Design, 303-830-6855; **www.babylonfloral.com**

**Botanical Wonderland**
Oregon Flower Growers Association/Portland Flower Market, 503-289-1500 x 4; **www.pdxflowermarket.com/ofga**

Lavish, 503-228-1558; **www.lavishflora.com**

Artis + Greene, 503-957-9567; **www.artisplusgreene.com**

Solabee Flowers and Botanicals, 503-307-2758; **www.solabeeflowers.com**

ink & peat, 503-282-6688; **www.inkandpeat.com**

**Organic Luxe**
Lily Lodge, 310-360-9400; **www.lilylodge.com**

**CHAPTER 3 (PAGES 88-103)**
**In a Paradise of Old Garden Roses**
For more information on finding old roses, visit **www.helpmefind.com/roses/ (V)**

**Eco-Friendly Flowers to Arrange Yourself**
Celadon & Celery, 646-833-7609; **www.celadoncelery.com**

**Shopping the Supermarket**
Ballard Market Floral Department, 206-783-7922;
**www.townandcountrymarkets.com**

**CHAPTER 4 (PAGES 104-129)**
**Julie & George Get Married**
*Sunset* magazine's gardens are open for self-guided walking tours from 9 a.m. to 4 p.m. Mondays through Fridays (except holidays). Sunset Headquarters, 80 Willow Rd., Menlo Park, CA 94025; Please call 650-321-3600 between 9 a.m. and 4 p.m. (Pacific Time) if you have questions; **www.sunset.com**

**Swoon-Inducing Dahlias**
Corralitos Gardens, 831-722-9952; **www.cgdahlias.com** (Note: Nursery hours vary; please call in advance to schedule a personal visit.)

**Ingredients for a Sunday Brunch**
Terra Bella Organic Floral, 206-783-0205; **www.terrabellaflowers.com (V)**

**Flowers for Chez Panisse**
Max Gill Design, 510-459-5831; **www.maxgilldesign.com**
Chez Panisse Restaurant & Cafe, 510-548-5525; **www.chezpanisse.com**

**CHAPTER 5 (PAGES 130-139)**
**From Their Fields to Your Vase**
Association of Specialty Cut Flower Growers, 440-774-2887; **www.ascfg.org**

Growing for Market, 800-307-8949; **www.growingformarket.com.** Lynn Byczynski authored *The Flower Farmer: An Organic Grower's Guide to Raising and Selling Cut Flowers* (Chelsea Green Publishing, 2008), recommended reading for aspiring commercial growers.

Dr. Allan Armitage, **www.allanarmitage.net**

Stems Cut Flowers, **www.stemscutflowers.com**

Flower Fields, **ngardner2@rochester.rr.com**

Tschetter's Flowers, **www.tschettersflowers.com**

# Acknowledgments

During our years of research and travel for this book, so many friends opened doors, housed and fed us, made introductions and shared encouragement and support. To the gardeners, farmers and designers who guided and inspired us, and to flower lovers everywhere for whom bouquets are more than just something ephemeral and fleeting – but instead an essential form of language – we say thank you.

Amy Stewart, our friend and fellow garden communicator, was an early supporter of this project. Her book *Flower Confidential* opened our eyes and gave us the motivation to further explore the world of local flowers. We are so grateful that she contributed this book's foreword.

Our friends Diane Szukovathy and Dennis Westphall of Jello Mold Farm have been perennial cheerleaders, encouragers and valuable resources. Similarly, Judy M. Laushman of the Association of Specialty Cut Flower Growers has supported our endeavors and given us a platform to share words and pictures in *The Cut Flower Quarterly.* And Mike Go, David's generous neighbor and friend, who has been one of our project's most loyal supporters, lent bunches of his favorite garden roses and countless hours of his expertise to shape and advise us on our blog, www.the50milebouquet.com.

Many editors over the years have said "yes" to Debra's story ideas about the field-to-vase movement, including Giselle Smith of *Seattle Homes & Lifestyles;* Julie Chai and Kathy Brenzel of *Sunset* magazine; Craig Nakano of the *Los Angeles Times;* Gayle Goodson Butler, Doug Jimerson and Eric Liskey of *Better Homes & Gardens;* and Margot Shaw of *flower* magazine. Several of those publications featured David's luscious photography of farmers, florists and flowers to illustrate the stories. Joe Lamp'l and Theresa Loe, our friends at "Growing a Greener World," produced an entire episode for their wonderful PBS show about this project. It was just the attention we needed at just the right time.

While creating this book, we also took to the road and lectured about the cultural shift to embrace local flowers, both together and at times individually. The seminar managers and education directors who invited us to speak, long before the idea of *The 50 Mile Bouquet* had become a reality, are our champions. We thank Gillian Mathews of Ravenna Gardens; Janet Endsley of the Northwest Flower & Garden Show; Lisa Moses of Molbak's Garden + Home; Celia Adamec, Leesly Leon, Sarah Olson and Matthew Cole of Denver Botanic Gardens; Beth Maurer of The Oregon Garden; Karen Kozol of the Woodinville Garden Club; Diane Threlkeld of the Jefferson County Master Gardeners; and Dawn Chaplin and Susann Schwiesow of the Whatcom Horticultural Society – and all the future venues on our lecture calendars.

Finally, we offer a huge bouquet of thanks to Paul Kelly, publisher of St. Lynn's Press, who totally "gets" our vision and took a creative risk to bring *The 50 Mile Bouquet* to the marketplace. Cathy Dees is a dream of an editor who gently and lovingly shaped the manuscript. And from the start, we counted ourselves incredibly fortunate to have James Forkner of Studio Bolo as our designer. He artfully combined Debra's words and David's images into the beautiful book you hold in your hand and we couldn't be happier.

# About the Author and Photographer

**Debra Prinzing** is a Seattle- and Los Angeles-based outdoor living expert who writes and lectures on gardens and home design. She has a background in textiles, journalism, landscape design and horticulture. A frequent speaker for botanical garden, horticultural society and flower show audiences, Debra is also a regular radio and television guest. Her five books include Garden Writers Association Gold Award-winning *Stylish Sheds and Elegant Hideaways* (Clarkson-Potter/Random House, 2008) and *The Abundant Garden* (Thomas Nelson Press, 2005).

Debra is a contributing garden editor for *Better Homes & Gardens* and her feature stories on architecture and design appear regularly in the Home section of the *Los Angeles Times.* She also contributes to *Garden Design, Organic Gardening, Horticulture, Fine Gardening, Cottages & Bungalows, Metropolitan Home, Landscape Architecture, Sunset, Alaska Airlines Magazine, Old House Interiors, flower* magazine, *Romantic Homes,* and others. Debra serves as president of the Garden Writers Association and was a co-founder of GreatGardenSpeakers.com. Learn more about Debra at: **www.debraprinzing.com.**

**David E. Perry** began exploring the world and telling stories with cameras on the day his father gave him a vintage Certo Dollina rangefinder and several rolls of film. It was his twelfth birthday. For much longer than that, he has actively sought reasons to have his hands buried in the dirt and his nose buried in bunches of flowers. In this book, he has found a way to combine those two great loves within one project.

To see other examples of his extensive photographic work or view his lecture and workshop topics, visit his web site at **www.davidperryphoto.com.** To follow along as he continues exploring the world of flowers and gardens through essays and pictures, you are invited to subscribe to his blog, A Photographer's Garden, at **http://davidperryphoto.com/blog.** You can also follow him on Twitter at **@DavidPerryPhoto.**

## About the Book

The idea for *The 50 Mile Bouquet,* chronicling the "slow flower" movement, began coming together in 2006. After corresponding with each other about the things we were each doing in our complementary spheres of garden writing and photography, we finally connected in person. Following an email exchange, we arranged a one-day road trip to the Skagit Valley to scout each other's garden sources, the highlight of which was a visit to the amazing heirloom rose garden of David's friend, Waverly Jaegel. That day we discovered (and continue to nurture) our mutual fascination with the stories of the floral industry's unsung heroes: the flower farmers.

This book has been years in the works, first as a concept, then as a self-funded creative collaboration. Along the way, the two of us delighted in each new encounter with a passionate grower or inventive floral designer – all of them believers in the importance of locally-grown and seasonal ingredients as their form of creative expression. The story of our winding *50 Mile Bouquet* "road trip" has been one of discovery and unforgettable beauty.

Visit Debra and David's web site and blog, **www.the50milebouquet.com,**
for more stories, interviews, photographs, videos and green floral design tips.

## Additional photo captions:

**Cover:** Wedding and event designer Stacie Sutliff of Blush Custom Floral (left) gains first-hand knowledge of floral design ingredients on a visit to one of her top suppliers, Diane Szukovathy of Jello Mold Farm (right).

**Title page and back cover:** David Perry's own windowsill arrangement of seven rustic bottles, each with a rose plucked from his backyard – an incredibly easy, yet elegant, "local" bouquet.

**Table of contents, left:** Gardeners love the vibrant red crocosmia for its dramatic architectural form – and floral designers delight in using it for fall arrangements after the petals drop and seed heads emerge.

**Table of contents, right, from top:** Allium 'Globemaster'; Waverly Jaegel holds a selection of her heirloom roses; apricot-hued foxtail lilies stand tall in Jan Roozen's fields, silhouetted against a fading red barn; a succulent echeveria and Dusty Miller foliage create a handsome boutonniere on groom George Lee's lapel; field-grown tulips, ready for harvesting; a simple nosegay of autumn blooming Kaffir lilies in a child's hand creates a storybook image; evoking timeless romance is a vase filled with *Rosa* 'Europeana', a floribunda rose in Mike Go's garden.